stitch

YOUR STORY

SIX COMPLETE ALPHABETS TO QUILT IN YOUR OWN WORDS

SARAH FIELKE

Published in 2019 by Lucky Spool Media, LLC
www.luckyspool.com
info@luckyspool.com

Text © Sarah Fielke
Editor: Susanne Woods
Designer: Rae Ann Spitzenberger
Illustrator: Kari Vojtechovsky
Photographer: Sue Stubbs
Photograph on page 59 reprinted by permission from The American Folk Art Museum/Art Resource, NY

9 8 7 6 5 4 3 2 1
First Edition
Printed in China

Library of Congress Cataloging-in-Publication Data available upon request

LSID0044

ISBN 978-1940655-35-2

CONTENTS

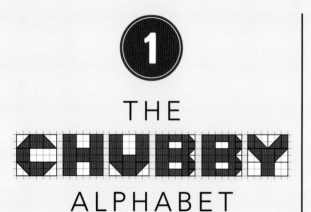

1

THE
CHUBBY
ALPHABET

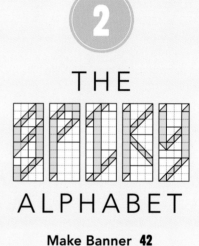

2

THE
BACKY
ALPHABET

3

THE
FORMAL
ALPHABET

THE
Back to Black
ALPHABET

THE

ALPHABET

THE
CURSIVE
BIAS TAPE
APPLIQUÉ
ALPHABET

INTRODUCTION

Ever since I started designing commercial patterns 20 years ago, I've looked for ways to put words in my quilts. Over the years I've played with lots of different methods, from appliqué to embroidery, fusible templates, piecing, foundation paper piecing, improv piecing, machine embroidery—you name it, I've done it! Many of the quilts incorporating text are some of my favorite quilts.

What fun for me to arrive at a place in quilting now where we are all loving the quilted word! 'Saying it' with fabric is such an individual and personal step in a quilt—it adds depth, meaning, humor, personality, feeling, a personal message, a political voice, a religious voice—or maybe just a fun way to showcase your favorite quote, song lyric or poem.

The great thing about fabric words, of course, is that they personalize everything, so don't think you're confined to a quilt top. 'Say it' on a cushion, a bag, a zip pouch, a pin cushion, a t-shirt, a curtain, the dog's bed…..

In this book, you will find a multitude of alphabets to help you have your say. The three pieced alphabets are traditionally pieced and created on a grid so that each letter can be resized to your own specifications by simply changing the size of each square in your grid. There's a cursive alphabet made for appliqué, a fun way to use bias tape, and my improv lettering technique, too. After many quilts-worth of piecing, improv is my favorite way ever to make quilty letters.

I hope each of you finds a favorite method of making your own words. I just can't wait to see what you make! If you use this book to make words from your stash, please share online on your social media platform of choice. I would LOVE to see!

THE

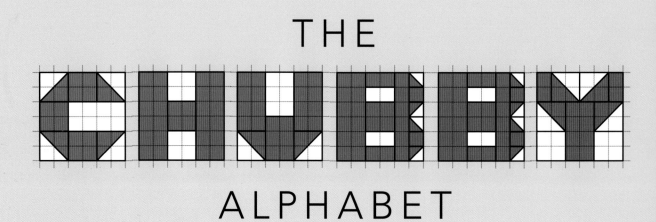

ALPHABET

LET'S PRACTICE!

THE CHUBBY ALPHABET

My first traditionally pieced, grid-based alphabet is called the Chubby Alphabet. Its chunky shape with angular lines makes this an ideal beginner-friendly alphabet to practice calculating gridwork. By simply changing the dimension of the grid square, the size of the finished letter blocks is entirely up to you! For example, these letters each finish at 6" if we assign a 1" dimension for each square of the grid. Not sure how that works? Don't worry! For each alphabet, we'll try some practice letters to get the hang of it, then you are free to experiment with changing the grid to produce your perfectly-sized message.

SIMPLER LETTERS

For practice, let's make each square in the grid equal 1". Therefore, our finished block is 6" (6½" unfinished).

TIP *Once you have determined the finished size you want your letters to be, remember to add the ½" for the seam allowance (¼" all the way around).*

So how do we calculate the size of pieces to cut for a letter? Let's start with an easy one: the letter 'T'. (Fig. 1)

Figure 1

The letter 'T' is made from four rectangles: two Letter fabric rectangles and two Background fabric rectangles. (Fig. 2)

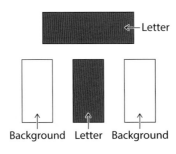

← Letter

Background   Letter   Background

Figure 2

The horizontal top of the 'T' is the full width of the block. Because we are working on a 1" grid square (6" finished block), we calculate the cut size of the top of the 'T' to be 6" wide finished, 6½" cut:

6 x 1" = 6", plus ½" seam allowance (¼" all the way around)

The top is two squares high:

2" + ½" seam allowance = 2½"

So, the top rectangle is 6½" x 2½" cut. (Fig. 3)

Figure 3

The three vertical bottom rectangles are each the same size.

2 squares x 4 squares = 2½" x 4½" cut

You will need to cut two Background rectangles this size, and one Letter fabric rectangle of the same size. (Fig. 4)

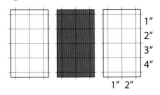

Figure 4

All the blocks are pieced together in rows, just as in traditional piecing. Our 'T' is made up of two rows: the top bar and the bottom vertical rectangles. (Fig. 5)

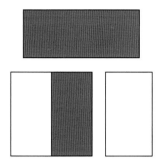

Figure 5

After the bottom row is sewn together, join it along the length of the top rectangle to complete the letter. (Fig. 6)

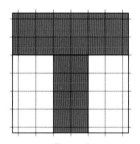

Figure 6

An uppercase letter 'T'!

The adjustability in this alphabet lies in changing the size of the grid square to suit your project. For example, if each square in the grid was assigned a measurement of 2", you would have 6 squares x 2" = 12" finished, plus your seam allowance, for 12" letter blocks, so 12½" unfinished. If each square in the grid was assigned a measurement of ½", you would have 6 squares x ½" = 3" finished, plus your seam allowance, for 3" letter blocks, so 3½" unfinished.

MORE COMPLEX LETTERS

Was that too easy? Let's try a harder one. The uppercase letter 'P' has some smaller rectangles and some triangles, but it is calculated in the same way as our 'T'. (Fig. 7)

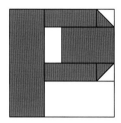

Figure 7

It goes together in one solid column and four rows. (Fig. 8)

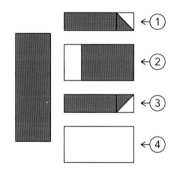

Figure 8

Let's start with the column. We have met this size before with the horizontal row of the uppercase 'T', but this time use a vertical rectangle for the uppercase 'P':

2½" x 6½" including seam allowance (¼" all the way around)

Rows 1 and 3 are Letter fabric rectangles of 3 squares x 1 square, plus a 1" half-square triangle (or HST for short):

(1) 3½" x 1½" rectangle + a 1½" unfinished HST unit

For ease of calculating the triangles in this alphabet, use the one-at-a-time method for creating HSTs.

TIP *Feel free to use your favorite HST method by finding the finished size of the triangle unit first using the grid and then adding the seam allowance.*

To make triangles from a square, add ⅞" to the finished grid square size. So, for our 'P' where each square on the grid measures 1" finished, cut a 1⅞" square first, then cut the square in half on the diagonal to yield the triangles needed for that size HST.

Cut the 1⅞" squares of Letter and Background fabric in half on the diagonal. Stitch one Background fabric triangle to one Letter fabric triangle along the long side. Press and trim the little "dogears" off the square, and you will have a 1½" HST(1" finished). (Fig. 9)

Figure 9

Continue to calculate the cut size of the units in each row. Cut and sew them together in rows, then add the vertical column. The uppercase 'P'!

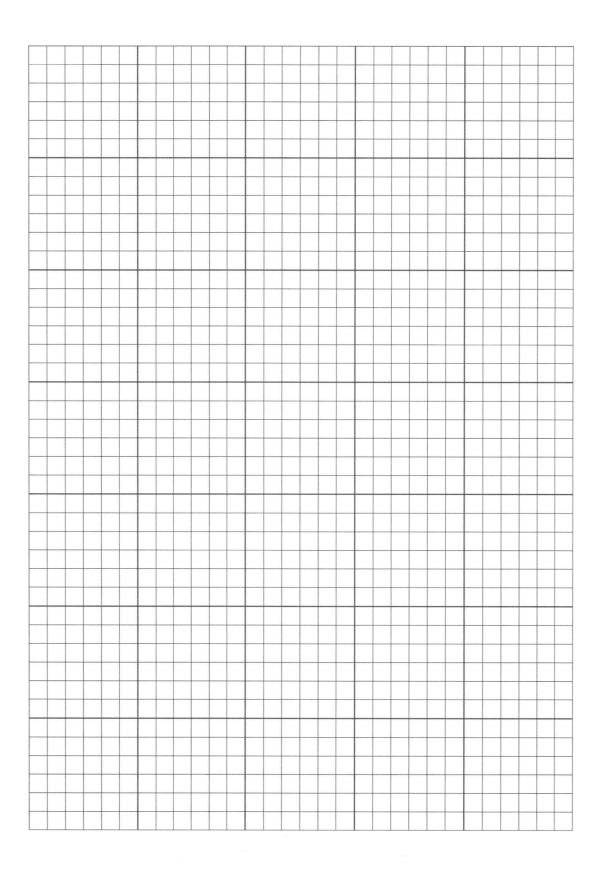

GRIDWORK

Learning to use a grid like this for patchwork is a huge asset. All you need to do is assign each square a finished measurement and multiply that measurement by 6 to get the finished size of your block. Again, remember to add the seam allowance to each piece after you have calculated its finished size. Master this math, and you can make these Chubby Alphabet letters the perfect size to suit any project.

All the lowercase letters in the Chubby Alphabet are calculated in the same way. I want to walk you through is the uppercase 'E' as well. In order to get the 'E' in a pleasing proportion, use some half and quarter-squares on the grid. You will see that the top, middle and bottom legs of the front of the 'E' are 1½ squares wide, and the space between is ¾ of a square. (Fig. 10)

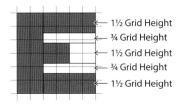

Figure 10

To calculate this, perform exactly the same math. For example, sticking with a 1" grid, 1½ squares calculate as 1½", plus the ½" seam allowance to make a 2" cut.

Determining the cut size of the space between uses the same method, ¾ of a square is ¾", plus ½" seam allowance to make a 1¼" cut. The 'G' also uses partial squares. (Fig. 11)

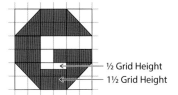

Figure 11

Armed with all this knowledge, you can now make the projects in this chapter using the Chubby Alphabet (see pages 14–15) and photocopy the grid on the facing page to design your own words for a project.

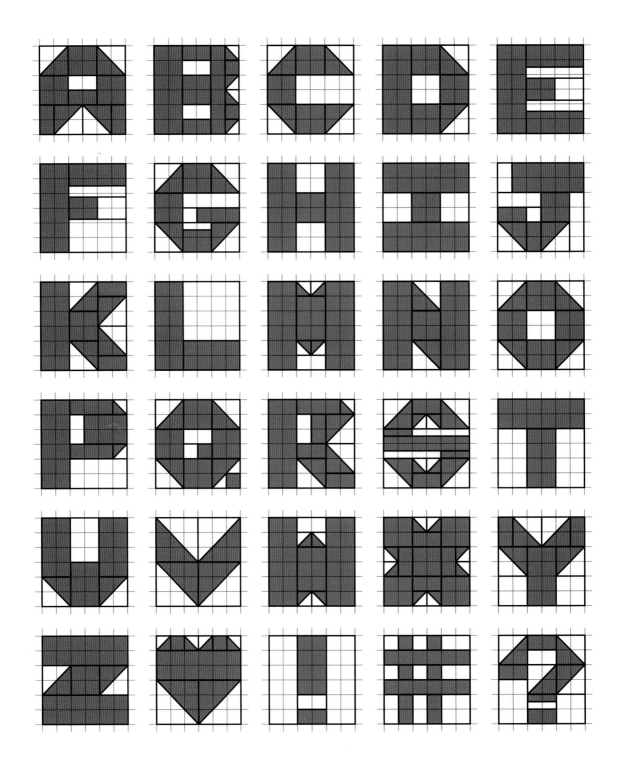

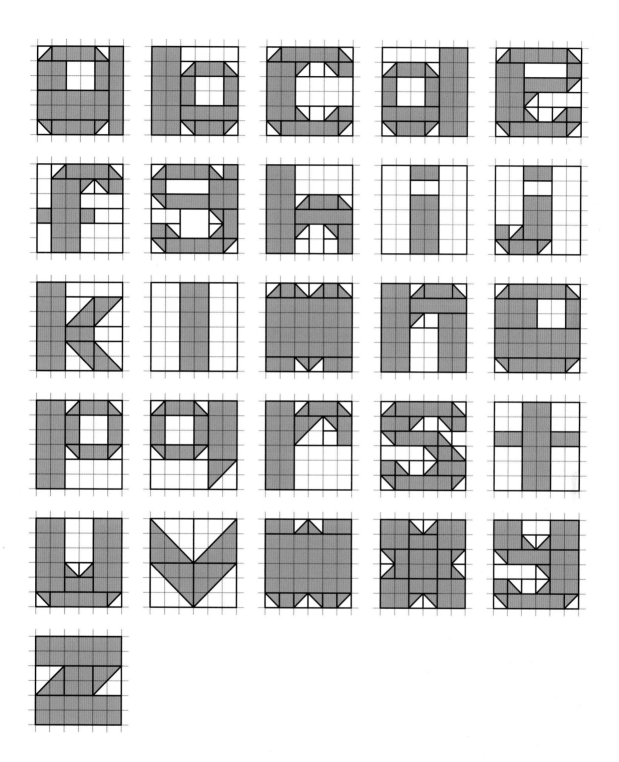

'KNIT THIS' BUCKET BAG

A bucket bag with handles that is large enough to hold a sweater's worth of yarn, is a knitting must-have. Mine says 'KNIT THIS' but you can personalize yours to say anything that takes your fancy. Just make sure that your exterior panel measurements are the same as mine, so that the other measurements are accurate!

The exterior of this bag is made using the Chubby Alphabet letters (see pages 14–15). The finished size here is based on using 1" grid squares that we practiced earlier (see page 10). This means the letter blocks are 6" finished, 6½" unfinished.

Finished Size: 11" wide x 20" high x 11" deep (28cm x 51cm x 28 cm)

MATERIALS

½ yard (45cm x Width of Fabric) of Exterior Fabric

¼ yard (25cm x WOF) of Collar Fabric

4" (10cm x WOF) x each of 8 Letter Fabrics

4" (10cm) x WOF of Handle Fabric

1 yard (70cm x WOF) of Lining Fabric

(1) 36" x 26" (90cm x 65cm) rectangle of foam Stabilizer, such as ByAnnie's Soft and Stable foam (or similar)

(1) 42" (1.05m) length of ½" Cording

Basting spray

Sharp pencil

Walking foot (optional)

Safety pin or bodkin

CUTTING

From the Exterior Fabric, cut:
(1) 11½" square for the Base

(2) 5¼" x 12½" rectangles

(1) 34" x 1½" rectangle

From the Stabilizer, cut:
(1) 34" x 13½" rectangle for the Exterior

(1) 11½" square for the Base

(2) 1½" x 16" rectangles for the Handles

From the Lining Fabric, cut:
(1) 34" x 13½" rectangle

1 circle from the Knit This Bag Pattern A (see page 21)

(2) 17¼" x 7½" rectangles

From the Handle Fabric, cut:
(2) 4" x 16" rectangles

From the Collar Fabric, cut:
(2) 17¼" x 7½"rectangles

Use a ¼" seam allowance unless otherwise noted.

PIECING THE EXTERIOR PANEL

1 Refer to the Chubby Alphabet (see pages 14–15) and the grid (see page 16), to calculate and cut the pieces required from the Letter fabrics and remaining Exterior fabric. Make one 'K', 'N', 'H' and 'S', and two 'T's and 'I's, each as 6½" unfinished blocks.

2 Sew the letters together into two separate rows: K-N-I-T in one row and T-H-I-S in the other. Press. (Fig. 1)

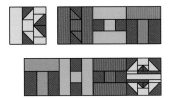

Figure 1

3 With the right sides facing, sew the KNIT row to the top of the THIS row. Press.

4 Sew a 5¼" x 12½" Exterior rectangle to each short side of the assembled panel from Step 3 and press. Attach the 34" x 1½" Exterior rectangle to the bottom of the panel. The assembled Exterior Panel will now measure 34" x 13½". Press well. (Fig. 2)

Figure 2

QUILTING

1 Following the manufacturer's instructions and working in a well-ventilated area, spray the wrong side of the Exterior and Base stabilizer pieces with basting spray. Smooth the Assembled Exterior Panel and the 11½" Base square onto the stabilizer with the right sides of the fabrics facing up.

2 Quilt the basted units as desired. I machine quilted horizontal lines ¼" apart over the Exterior Panel and a crosshatch pattern 2" apart onto the Base. Press.

> **TIP** *If you are machine quilting, I recommend using a walking foot if you have one, so that your fabric moves smoothly under your machine.*

3 Using the Pattern A circle on page 21, cut out a circle from the quilted Base from Step 2.

ASSEMBLING THE EXTERIOR

1 Fold the quilted Exterior Panel in half with the right sides together, and stitch along the short raw edges creating a tall cylinder. The right sides of the exterior fabric are facing inwards. Press the seam open as best you can—it's a little fiddly with the foam. If this is a struggle, try carefully trimming away the foam inside the seam allowance to a scant ¼". (Fig. 3)

Figure 3

2 Fold the cylinder in half so it lies flat, with the seam centered and facing up. Using pins, mark both folds along the bottom raw edge of the cylinder. This will help with alignment later.

3 Unfold the cylinder and re-fold in half with the seam on one side and repeat Step 2. These pins mark the four quarters of the bottom of the Exterior Panel.

4 Fold the Base in half to create a crease, marking with pins at both ends of the fold. Unfold and bring the pinned points together to fold in half, gently finger pressing to create another crease. Pin at both folded ends to define the four quarters for the Base.

5 With the right sides facing, align the quarter-mark pins of the Base to those of the Exterior Panel. Pin along the raw edges, easing as you go if you need to. This can be fiddly, so using lots of pins or clips will make it easier. (Fig. 4)

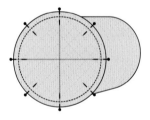

Figure 4

6 Position the pinned cylinder on its end and stitch around the circumference of the Base to attach it to the cylinder.

ASSEMBLING THE LINING

Repeat Steps 1–6 from Assembling the Exterior with the Lining rectangle and Lining Base, but leave a 6" gap in the side seam of the Lining, for turning later. Be sure to backstitch at the beginning and end of each line of stitching. (Fig. 5)

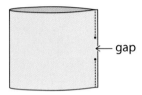

← gap

Figure 5

ASSEMBLING THE HANDLES

1 On the wrong side of a Handle rectangle, measure and mark a line ½" away from both long edges.

2 Fold one long edge over to the wrong side on the drawn line and press. (Fig. 6)

Figure 6

3 Following the manufacturer's instructions, apply basting spray to both sides of a Stabilizer Handle rectangle. Align one edge of the foam with the remaining visible ½" line. Fold the loose half-inch of fabric over the Stabilizer, and firmly stick in place. (Fig. 7)

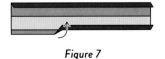

Figure 7

4 Fold the remaining fabric over the stabilizer, aligning the two folded edges to snugly enclose the foam.

5 Edgestitch through all the layers along both long sides, making sure to catch the two folded edges in the stitching to secure the Handle closed.

Figure 8

6 Repeat Steps 1–5 to create the second Handle.

ATTACHING THE HANDLES

1 Determine the center of the bag on the assembled Exterior cylinder and fold in half with the center point facing up. Mark the center at the top raw edge of the side folds of the bag with pins. Unfold the cylinder and position one short end of a Handle 3½" away from either side of the center front pin, aligning the raw edges. Pin and baste in place using a ⅛" seam allowance. (Fig. 9)

Figure 9

2 Repeat with the remaining Handle, aligning it 3½" away from the opposite pin from Step 1.

ASSEMBLING AND ATTACHING THE COLLAR

1 Position a 17¼" x 7½" Collar and Lining rectangle right sides together. Sew along one long edge and press the seam open. Repeat with the remaining Collar and Lining rectangles.

2 Position the assembled units from Step 1 right sides facing, matching up the Collar and Lining fabrics. Stitch along one short edge. Repeat for the opposite short edge, but this time leave a 1" gap on the Collar rectangle, 1¼" from the center seam. Be sure to backstitch at either side of the gap. (Fig. 10)

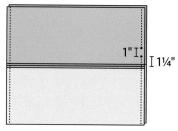

Figure 10

3 Press the seams open. Turn the Collar right side out and stitch a rectangle around the gap in the side seam, about ⅛" from the opening. This secures the seam allowances in place and creates the casing opening. (Fig. 11)

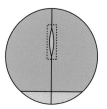

Figure 11

4 Fold the Lining and the Collar fabrics wrong sides facing, aligning the bottom raw edges. Press along the fold. This is now the top edge of the bag. Edgestitch ¼" away from the fold.

5 Using a ruler and a sharp pencil, measure and draw one line ¾" away and a second line 1¾" away from the stitching in Step 4. These marked lines should overlap your stitching around the casing opening from Step 3 (Fig. 12). Sew on the marked lines. Turn the Collar so that the Collar Lining is facing out.

Figure 12

FINISHING

1 Slip the assembled Collar over the Exterior Panel with the Exteriors facing. Align the gap in the Collar seam with the back center of the Exterior Panel and align the raw edges. Use a few pins to hold the layers in place. (Fig. 13)

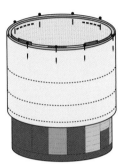

Figure 13

2 With the Lining wrong side out, position the pinned Exterior/Collar unit from Step 1 inside the Lining cylinder. You may have to fold the Exterior up a bit to get this to happen without a struggle! Align the Lining and Exterior seams and the raw edges of all the layers.

3 Pin along the raw edges, then stitch around the entire circumference of the bag. (Fig. 14)

> **TIP** *Since your bag may carry large projects and there are so many layers of fabric here, I recommend sewing a reinforcing row of zigzag or overlock stitches around this seam for added strength.*

4 Turn the bag right side out through the gap in the Lining. Again, this will be a bit of a push and shove, but persist!

5 Push the Lining inside the bag and press the Collar and Handles up and away from the bag. Topstitch through all the layers along the seam where the Collar and the Exterior Panel meet, with the Handles facing upwards towards the Collar. This will make them stand up nicely and not fall down over the bag.

6 Put a safety pin or bodkin through one end of the Cording and feed it through the casing in the Collar. Start at the casing opening and working all the way around, pulling the safety pin out through the same opening. Tie a large knot at each end of the Cording so it can't get lost inside the casing and trim the ends neatly.

7 Hand slipstitch the gap in the Lining closed. Fill with yarn, draw the string and go find a shady tree to knit underneath!

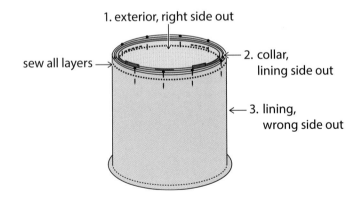

Figure 14

KNIT THIS BAG

Pattern A

Enlarge 175%

—— cut line

--- stitch line

seam allowance

'STITCH THAT' PROJECT BAG

The STITCH THAT letters are smaller than the 1" grid from the previous project and will give you some practice resizing your letters. Here, each square in the Chubby Alphabet square in the grid represents ¾", or 1¼" cut. This means our letters will be 4½" finished, 5" unfinished.

We'll also be using a different construction method for this bag, so be sure to read through the instructions carefully. *Note: This bag has no stabilizer, so requires no quilting.

Finished Size: 8½" wide x 13" high x 8½" deep (22cm x 33cm x 22 cm)

MATERIALS

16" (40cm) x WOF of Exterior Fabric

4" (10cm) x WOF each of 10 Letter Fabrics

12" (30cm) x WOF of Lining Fabric

10" (25cm) x WOF of Collar Fabric

(1) 32" (80cm) length of ½" Cording

(1) 10" (25cm) square of sturdy cardboard or template plastic for the Base support

CUTTING

From the Exterior Fabric, cut:
(2) 5" squares

1 using Pattern B (see page 122)

From the Cardboard, cut:
1 Base support using Pattern C (see page 123)

From the Lining Fabric, cut:
(1) 27½" x 9½" rectangle

1 circle using Pattern B (see page 122)

From the Collar Fabric, cut:
(4) 14" x 4½" rectangles or 2 from two different fabrics

Use a ¼" seam allowance unless otherwise noted.

PIECING THE EXTERIOR PANEL

1 Use the Letter fabrics and the remaining Exterior fabric to make one 'S', 'I', 'C' and 'A', two 'H's and four 'T's using the Chubby Alphabet (see pages 14–15) and based on a ¾" grid which yields 5" unfinished blocks.

2 Sew the letters together into two rows: S-T-I-T-C-H in one row and T-H-A-T in the other. Attach a 5" Exterior fabric square at each end of 'THAT' to make it the same length as 'STITCH'.

3 Stitch the two rows together into one Exterior Panel, which will measure 27½" wide x 9½" high. (Fig. 1)

Figure 1

ASSEMBLY

1 With the right sides facing, stitch the short ends of the Exterior together, forming a cylinder. Press the seam open and attach the Exterior Base following Steps 1–6 of Assembling the Exterior in the KNIT THIS Bucket (see page 18). Turn the assembled Exterior right side out.

2 Repeat using the Lining rectangle and Lining Base to create the assembled Lining, sewing the entire side seam as for the Exterior.

3 Assemble the Collar following Steps 1–3 of Assembling and Attaching the Collar in the KNIT THIS Bucket (see page 19).

4 Fold the raw edge of the Lining half of the Collar ¼" to the wrong side. Press. (Fig. 2)

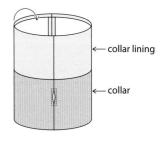

← collar lining

← collar

Figure 2

FINISHING

1 With the assembled Exterior right side out, insert the Base support cardboard circle into the base of the bag. If needed, trim the cardboard so it fits neatly in place.

2 Slip the Lining inside the Exterior, so the wrong sides are together, and align the seam and the top raw edges. Pin the layers together and baste along the raw edges using a ⅛" seam allowance.

3 With the wrong side of the assembled Collar facing out, slip the Collar over the top of the unit from Step 1 and align the raw edges at the top. The Collar should not be folded in half; it should be open with the folded edge down at the bottom. Stitch through all the layers along the raw edges.

4 Pull the Collar up and away from the bag and press the seam between the Exterior and the Collar towards the Collar itself. Fold the Collar in half so that the wrong sides are now facing and press the topmost seam so it is nice and sharp. Edgestitch ¼" from the fold.

> **TIP** *You may want to pin the layers of the Collar together between these steps, but be careful that they don't get in the way of the stitching needed to form the casing.*

5 Using a ruler and a sharp pencil, draw a line 1" away from the stitching in Step 3 continuing all the way around the Collar. This marked line should overlap the stitching around the casing opening. Sew on the marked line to create a casing.

6 Pin the folded edge of the Collar that is still loose inside the bag neatly to the bag Lining. With the bag right side out, stitch along the seam between the Collar and the Exterior Panel, securing the folded edge in place on the Lining. This will provide a nice finish on the outside of the bag at the same time.

7 Using a safety pin or bodkin, thread one end of the Cording through the drawstring opening and feed it through the casing in the Collar. Work all the way around, and pull the safety pin out through the same opening. Tie a large knot at the end of each length of Cording and trim neatly.

Pack up your cross-stitch and put the kettle on.

RELAX CUSHION SET

Cushions are a really fun way to incorporate something you want to say into your home. I have a favorite spot where I like to stitch or read. These cushions live there, reminding all who pass by to stop, breathe and take a moment to r e l a x....

The letters are created using a grid system and the Chubby Alphabet (see pages 14–15). Each square in the grid measures 2". To give the letters the impression of floating on a patchwork surface, the background squares measure 3" (3½" cut).

Finished Pillow Size: 18" (45cm) square each

MATERIALS
NOTE The materials listed below create five cushions.

¾ yard (70cm) Letter Fabric

1⅓ yards (1.2m) total of at least 5 different Background Fabrics

1⅞ yards (1.7m) Backing Fabric

2¾ yards (2.5m) lightweight woven fusible Interfacing, 20" (50cm) wide

10½ yards (9.6m) of ¼" corded Piping (optional)

(5) 20" (50cm) square cushion inserts

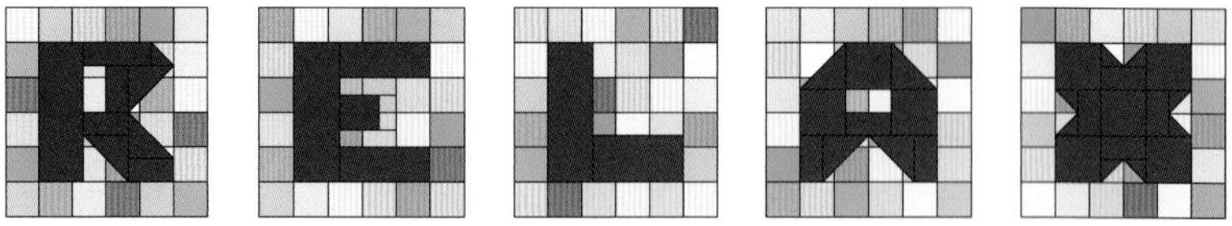

CUTTING
From the assorted Background Fabrics, cut:
a total of at least (118) 3½" squares

From the Backing Fabric, cut:
(5) 18½" x 10½" rectangles

(5) 18½" x 14½" rectangles

From the Interfacing, cut:
(5) 18½" squares

For the Letter 'R'
From the Letter Fabric, cut:
(1) 4½" x 12½" rectangle

(1) 6½" x 2½" rectangle

(3) 4½" x 2½" rectangles (2 horizontal and 1 vertical)

3 triangles cut from 4⅞" squares

1 triangle cut from a 2⅞" square

From the Background Fabrics, cut:
(1) 2½" x 3½" rectangle

(1) 2½" x 1½" rectangle

3 pieced triangles cut from a 4-Patch (see page 26)

1 triangle cut from the modified instructions on page 26 for under the 'R'

1 triangle cut from a 2⅞" square

For the Letter 'E'
From the Letter Fabric, cut:
(1) 4½" x 12½" rectangle

(2) 8½" x 3½" rectangles

(1) 4½" x 3½" rectangle

From the Background Fabrics, cut:
(2) 3½" x 2" rectangles

(2) 2" squares in matching fabric to the rectangles above

(2) 2½" x 2" rectangles

For the Letter 'L'
From the Letter Fabric, cut:
(1) 4½" x 12½" rectangle

(1) 8½" x 4½" rectangle

From the Background Fabrics, cut:
(4) 3½" x 2½" rectangles (2 horizontal and 2 vertical)

(1) 2½" square

For the Letter 'A'
From the Letter Fabric, cut:
(3) 4½" squares

4 triangles cut from 4⅞" squares

(3) 2½" x 4½" rectangles

From the Background Fabrics, cut:
(2) 2½" squares

4 pieced triangles from two 4-Patch units (see page 26)

For the Letter 'X'
From the Letter Fabric, cut:
(5) 4½" squares

8 triangles cut from 2⅞" squares

(4) 2½" x 4½" rectangles (2 horizontal and 2 vertical— or if preferred to minimize piecing, 2 horizontal and 1 larger 8½" x 4½" rectangle and cut one fewer 4½" square)

From the Background Fabrics, cut:
8 triangles cut from 2⅞" squares

Use a ¼" seam allowance unless otherwise noted.

MAKING PIECED TRIANGLES

1 Sew (4) 3½" Background squares together to make a 4-Patch unit. (Fig. 1)

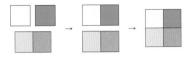

Figure 1

2 Measure 4⅞" away from a corner in each direction. You can also use a triangle ruler or the 45-degree line on an acrylic ruler if you have one. Cut the corner off the 4-Patch, resulting in a pieced triangle the same size as the Letter triangles cut from the 4⅞" squares. Repeat on the opposite corner of the 4-Patch. (Fig. 2)

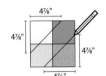

Figure 2

3 Repeat Steps 1 and 2 to make a total of six pieced 4-Patch triangles, four for the 'A' and two for the 'R'. (Fig. 3)

Figure 3

4 The pieced triangle that sits under the letter 'R' is made in the same manner, but the seams are in a slightly different position to align with the border squares. From the Background fabric, cut one 2½" x 3½" rectangle, one 3" square, and one 2½" square.

5 Sew the 2½" square to the top of the rectangle, press, and sew the 3" square to the side of the unit as shown.

R triangle piecing

6 Cut a 4⅞" triangle from the bottom left hand corner of the piece as shown.

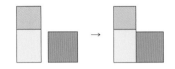

R triangle cutting

PIECING THE LETTERS

1 Piece the 12" finished letter blocks first, using the Chubby Alphabet instructions on pages 14–15. For example, for the letter 'L', assemble the inner Background pieces first. (Fig. 4)

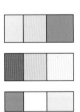

Figure 4

2 Attach the bottom leg of the 'L'. (Fig. 5)

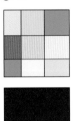

Figure 5

3 Next, attach the long side of the 'L'. (Fig. 6)

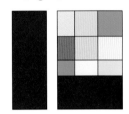

Figure 6

4 For 'R', 'A', and 'X', sew the pieced and cut triangles into squares, then continue to construct the blocks.

5 Add a column of four 3½" Background squares to the opposite sides of the letter to make the side borders. (Fig. 7)

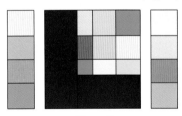

Figure 7

6 Finally, attach a row of six Background 3½" squares for the top and bottom borders. (Fig. 8)

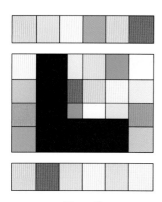

Figure 8

ASSEMBLING THE CUSHIONS

1 Following the manufacturer's instructions, fuse an 18" square of Interfacing to the wrong side of each pieced cushion Front. Trim if needed to square-up. If using Piping, baste the Piping to the right side of the cushion Front, using a ¼" seam allowance, overlapping the ends at the center of the bottom edge of each pillow. Trim the ends after basting.

2 Make a double hem on one 18½" side of each of your Backing rectangles by folding one 18½" edge in ¼" and pressing with an iron. Fold the edge in another ¼" and press. Topstitch ⅛" away from the folded edge and press. (Fig. 9)

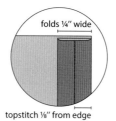

folds ¼" wide

topstitch ⅛" from edge

Figure 9

3 Lay your finished pillow Front right side facing up. With the right sides together, align a 18½" x 14½" Backing rectangle with three raw edges of the pillow Front. (Fig. 10)

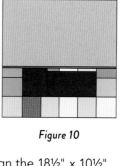

Figure 10

4 Align the 18½" x 10½" Backing rectangle along the opposite edge of the pillow Front. The Backing rectangles will overlap. (Fig. 11)

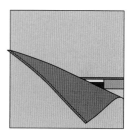

Figure 11

5 Pin around all four sides and sew using a ¼" seam. Trim the corners to remove some of the bulk, being careful not to cut into the seam.

6 Turn the pillow right side out, press, and place a 20" square pillow insert inside the pillow sleeve.

> **TIP** *Using a slightly larger pillow form than your finished cushion sleeve will help your pillow keep its shape over time.*

7 Repeat Steps 2–6 for a total of five cushions and … relax.

WHAT GOES AROUND

This quilt is made using the Chubby Alphabet, so be sure to use the instructions provided (see pages 14–15) to piece the letters. For this project they are all 6" finished which means that each grid square measures 1". Of course, I've designed these projects to accommodate your own special word or phrase, so you may decide to work on a pattern that uses a larger or smaller grid size.

To help you get started, I have included piecing diagrams for the L-O-V-E letters and the heart block. Don't forget to check back to the grid instructions for details on how to cut your HSTs (see page 11)!

My version of this quilt is pieced very scrappily, despite the color palette being cohesive. If you would like a similar look, I suggest cutting all the letter 'L's first, then all the letter 'O's etc., and using pieces of all the same fabrics to sew a few of each letter. Then mix up the fabrics within the word so you end up with lots of different fabrics pieced into each L-O-V-E.

Finished Size: 90" (225cm) square

MATERIALS

¾ yard (70cm) each of 10–12 Background Fabrics

¾ yard (70cm) each of 10–15 Background Letter Fabrics

4" (10cm) x WOF of each of 20 different Contrast Letter Fabrics

4" (10cm) x WOF Contrast Heart Fabric

⅞ yard (80cm) Binding Fabric

8¼ yards (7.5m) Backing Fabric, or 2¾ yds (2.45m) of 108" wideback Backing fabric

98" (2.45m) square of Batting

CUTTING

See the uppercase letters on page 14 to determine cut sizes.

From the Background Fabric, cut pieces for:

41 Letter 'L' blocks

45 Letter 'O' blocks

41 Letter 'V' blocks

43 Letter 'E' blocks

41 Heart blocks

2 Letter 'R' blocks

2 Letter 'D' blocks

1 of each of Letter 'M', 'A', 'K', 'S', 'T', 'H', 'W', 'G', 'U', 'N' blocks

From the Background Letter Fabric, cut pieces for:

40 Letter 'L' blocks

42 Letter 'O' blocks

41 Letter 'V' blocks

41 Letter 'E' blocks

40 Heart blocks

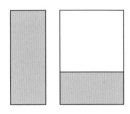

'L' Block Assembly

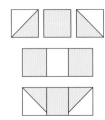

'O' Block Assembly

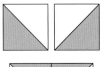

'V' Block Assembly

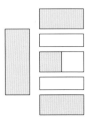

'E' Block Assembly

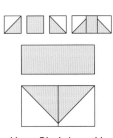

Heart Block Assembly

From the Contrast Letter
Fabric, cut sections for:
   2 of each of Letter 'R', 'D', 'E'
   blocks

   3 Letter 'O' blocks

   1 of each of Letter 'M', 'A', 'K',
   'S', 'T', 'H', 'W', 'L', 'G', 'U', 'N'
   blocks

From the Contrast Heart Fabric,
cut sections for:
   1 Heart block

From the Binding fabric, cut:
   (10) 3" x WOF strips

Use a ¼" seam allowance unless
otherwise noted.

PIECING THE BLOCKS

Piece the letter and heart
blocks according to the
directions in the grid section
of this alphabet and the
diagrams on the facing page.

ASSEMBLING THE QUILT TOP

1 On a flat surface or design
wall if you have one, arrange
the finished blocks into a grid
of 15 rows of 15 blocks each.
Use the Assembly Diagram
(page 31) as a guide for block
placement.

   TIP *To achieve the
   random, staggered effect,
   be mindful not to begin
   every row with the 'L'.
   This contributes to the
   effect that the grey LOVE
   blocks are providing the
   background, and the red
   blocks will stand out as
   their own words. If all of
   the grey LOVE blocks in the
   background were identical
   in placement, the red
   words would not read as
   clearly.*

2 Beginning with the top row, stitch all 15 blocks together. Repeat with all 15 rows, pressing the seams in alternate directions for each row so the seams will nest. When you have pieced all 15 rows, stitch the rows together, taking care to align the nested seams carefully. Press.

FINISHING

Layer the Backing rectangle with the wrong side up, then the Batting, and finally the quilt top right side up. Baste, quilt, and attach the binding using your favorite method.

QUILTING

I had WHAT GOES AROUND machine quilted in straight lines, ½" apart. The letters are quilted alternately horizontally, and then vertically. The machine quilting was done by Kat Jones. I hand quilted ¼" inside seams on the contrast letters using red thread. The chunky, linear structure of these blocks all grouped together in rows, lends itself to a modern quilting design of lines and grids. Alternately, a loose edge-to-edge pattern of hearts could blend into the background too and not overpower the patchwork.

1 ←
2 ←
3 ←
4 ←
5 ←
6 ←
7 ←
8 ←
9 ←
10 ←
11 ←
12 ←
13 ←
14 ←
15 ←

Assembly Diagram

THE

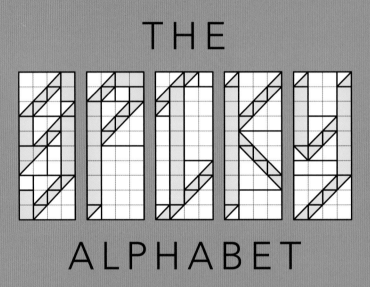

ALPHABET

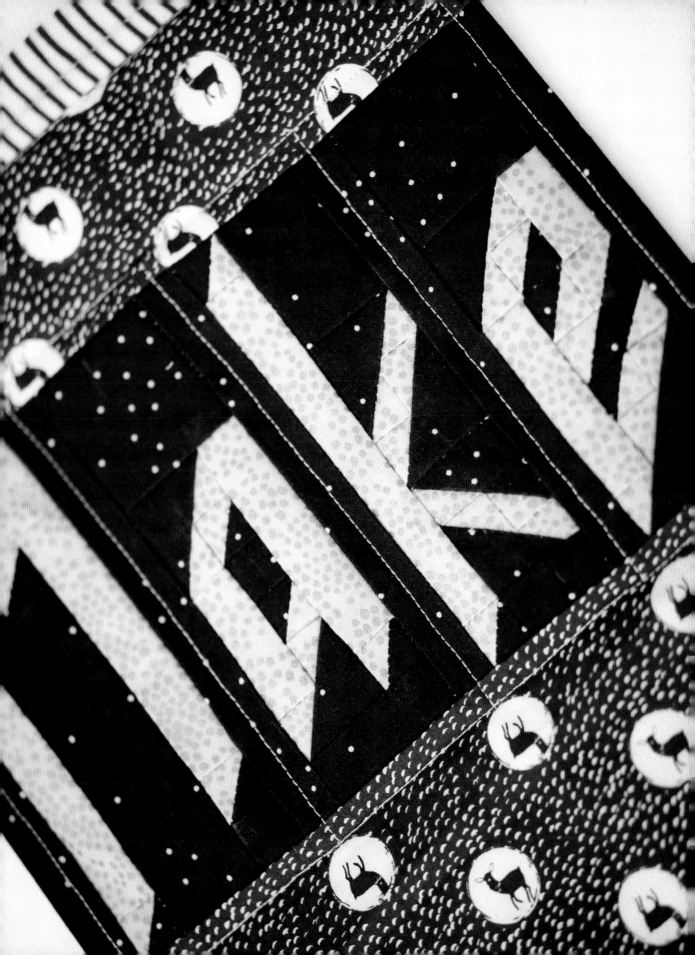

LET'S PRACTICE!
THE SPIKY ALPHABET

Our second traditionally-pieced, grid-based alphabet is called the *Spiky Alphabet*. It's full of lovely slanty shapes and pointy ends, very different from the cute, squat Chubby Alphabet letters. This alphabet isn't quite as adjustable, as the letters are already pretty large at 10" finished height using a 1" grid. I specifically designed this to be the star of the show in any quilt. So, if you are looking for something long, slim and elegant, this is the style for you!

Due to the slant of the letters, this alphabet is also a little trickier to piece. There are lots of HSTs and small pieces to cut and sew, but I promise that the end result is well worth the effort and makes a big impact.

SIMPLE LETTERS

Calculate the finished and cut size of the letter and background pieces in the same manner as we did for the Chubby Alphabet; however, some of the letters have quite a few smaller sections to make before they can be sewn into blocks, and some even use a different construction method entirely. Ready to dive in? Let's practice an easy letter: the letter 'A'.

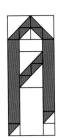

Spiky Alphabet letter 'A'

1 The uppercase 'A' is made in four sections that are then sewn together to form the 4" x 10" finished block. (Fig. 1)

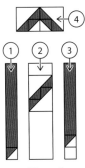

Figure 1

2 Sections 1 and 3 are straightforward. For Section 1, piece seven squares long by one square wide. Using a 1" grid square, that's 1" x 7", plus the seam allowance. So the rectangle of Letter fabric is 1½" x 7½".

TIP *Make the HST units in the same manner as the Chubby Alphabet (see page 11) by adding ⅞" to the finished size to calculate the cut size of the square, then cutting that square in half along the diagonal. You may decide to sew the small HSTs a bit larger than needed, press and then trim them to size for a perfect fit.*

3 To create the 1" square HST, cut a 1⅞" square from both the Letter and the Background fabrics. Cut both in half along the diagonal, and stitch each pair of fabric triangles together on the long edge. Sew the HST to the bottom of the rectangle from Step 2, being sure that the Letter fabrics are forming the correct angles. (Fig. 2)

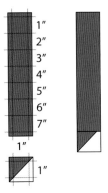

Figure 2

4 Repeat Steps 1–3 for Section 3 using a 6-square rectangle (1½" x 6½" cut), a 1-square HST (1½" assembled, unfinished), and a 1-square (1½" cut) Background square. (Fig. 3)

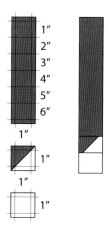

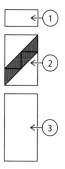

Figure 3

5 Section 2 is made from three sections. (Fig. 4)

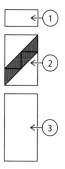

Figure 4

6 Cut a 2-square x 1-square Background rectangle (2½" x 1½", cut) for the top, and a 2-square x 4-square Background rectangle (2½" x 4½", cut) for the bottom of Section 3.

7 For the middle section, you will need two Background triangles that are 2-squares (a 2⅞" square cut in half on the diagonal), plus (4) 1-square triangles from the Letter fabric (a pair of 1⅞" squares cut in half on the diagonal). (Fig. 5)

Figure 5

8 Sew the triangles together along the straight sides in pairs (Figs. 6–7). Press and trim off the "dogears" and sew two pairs together, aligning the sides to make a diagonal line.

TIP *I highly recommend arranging the triangles on a flat surface before sewing to ensure the proper alignment of this section. Be careful when you press them not to stretch the bias edges on the triangles. (Figs. 6–7)*

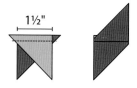

1½"

Figure 6

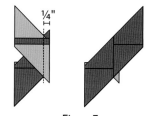

¼"

Figure 7

9 Sew (1) 2⅞" Background triangle to either side of the pieced strip from Step 8 to create a 2½" x 3½" rectangle. (Fig. 8)

Figure 8

10 Attach the Background rectangles from Step 6 to the top and bottom of the assembled unit from Step 9. (Fig. 9)

Figure 9

11 Sew Sections 1, 2 and 3 together along their 8½" length, press towards the Letter fabric and set aside.

12 For Section 4, make two 1-square Letter/Background HSTs. Sew the Letter triangles to the sides of the HSTs. Add a Background triangle to each and then sew the units together. (Fig. 10)

Figure 10

13 Sew Section 4 to the top of the assembled unit from Step 11 and you have your Spiky uppercase 'A'!

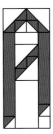

Completed A Block

COMPLEX LETTERS

Most of the letters in the Spiky Alphabet are pieced in exactly the same manner as the uppercase 'A'. Simply break down the grid into sections and straight lines, and you will be able to piece any of them with ease. The three exceptions in this alphabet are the uppercase 'X' and 'Z', and the lowercase 'x'. These letters are trickier to fit into our grid.

THE LETTER 'X'

1 To make the uppercase 'X', cut (1) 4½" x 10½" Background rectangle and (2) 1½" x 12½" Letter strips. Cut the Background rectangle in half along the diagonal from bottom left to top right. (Fig. 11)

Figure 11

2 Find the center along the long side of a triangle and the center of the Letter strip. Pin with the wrong sides facing and stitch together. Press. The Letter strip will extend a bit beyond the triangle on both sides. Repeat with the second triangle.

3 Use the center point of the Letter strip to align your ruler and trim the assembled rectangle from Step 2 to 4½" x 10½". (Fig. 12)

Figure 12

4 Cut the trimmed unit from Step 3 along the opposite diagonal. (Fig. 13)

Figure 13

5 Align the center of the second Letter strip with the center of the Letter strip from one Step 4 unit, taking into account the ¼" seam allowance. Pin with the wrong sides facing and stitch together. The remaining Step 4 unit will not be centered on the Letter strip. Instead, match up the centers of both short legs of the 'X' across the longer Letter strip. Pin with the wrong sides facing and stitch. Repeat Step 3 to trim the finished block. (Fig. 14)

Figure 14

6 The lowercase 'x' is constructed using the same method. Start with a 4½" x 6½" Background rectangle and (2) 1½" x 8½" Letter fabric rectangles. Trim the assembled unit to 4½" x 6½" in Steps 3 and 5.

THE LETTER 'Z'

1 To make the uppercase 'Z', make (2) 1½" Letter/Background fabric HST squares as described on page 34.

2 Cut (2) 1½" x 3½" rectangles from the Letter fabric.

3 With the wrong sides facing, stitch an HST square from Step 1 to one short end of a Letter rectangle from Step 2. Press.

4 Repeat Step 3 with the remaining Letter rectangle and HST, this time attaching the HST to the opposite short end. (Fig. 15)

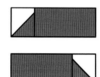

Figure 15

5 Cut a 4½" x 9½" Background rectangle. Subcut it from the bottom left hand corner to the top right hand corner, on the diagonal. (Fig. 16)

Figure 16

6 Cut a 1½" x 12" Letter strip. Find the center along the long side of a Background triangle from Step 5 and the center of the Letter strip. Pin with the wrong sides facing and stitch together. Press. The Letter strip will extend a bit beyond the triangle on both sides. Repeat with the second Background triangle on the opposite side of the Letter strip.

7 Trim the resulting rectangle to 4½" x 8½" in the same manner as for the uppercase 'X'. (Fig. 17)

Figure 17

8 Stitch the assembled units from Step 3 to the top and bottom of the unit from Step 7 paying attention to the orientation of the HSTs. Press. (Fig. 18)

Figure 18

VEERING FROM THE GRID

First, sketch out the word you would like to use in the alphabet as it appears in the master alphabet. You may find that your word doesn't look quite right. Let's explore some ideas for adjusting the grid to your liking.

Unlike the Chubby Alphabet, the Spiky Alphabet has uppercase letters that are taller than the lowercase. The wonderful thing about working with this particular alphabet in a grid is that the negative space around the lowercase letters allows for some adjustment. Think of those open spaces as being a place to slide your letters up and down to make a word that is visually pleasing to you, or that fits your project.

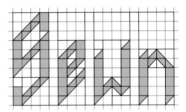

Example 1

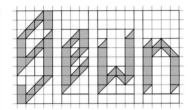

Example 2

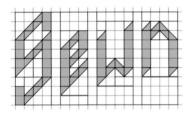

Example 3

For Example 1, the word 'Sewn' has been made exactly as it is shown in the master alphabet. It has negative space at the top of each letter but is aligned along the same gridline on the bottom of all the letters. It looks just like a traditional written or typed word, with all the letters balancing along the same base line.

In Example 2, I raised all the lowercase letters up by one square in the grid. This allows the uppercase letter 'S' to hang a little below them, which looks a bit more modern and funky. This offset alignment of the letters would alter the piecing of the negative spaces above and below each letter in our alphabet by a 1-square grid space.

In this last Example, all the letters are placed stepping up 1-square at a time, thus the letters are staggered. We are still working within our 10-square grid—I just slid everything up the scale! Obviously this won't always work (imagine for example that you had a lowercase 'f' in the middle of this word), but it's a fun option. If your word is longer, you could always keep stepping higher or lower out of the 10-square grid and just add some negative space to the top or bottom of the uppercase letter to compensate!

MODIFYING THE ALPHABET FOR THE ALWAYS QUILT

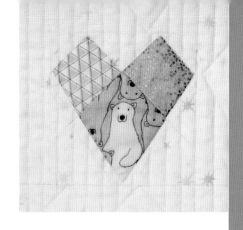

What happens when we introduce a letter with a tail, that would usually hang below the others, like a 'g' or, in this case, a 'y'?

For the project on page 46 the word 'Always' didn't look quite right to me. I'll walk you through some options I explored by sliding the letters along the grid so that you will see how flexible and fun this alphabet can be, depending on the desired end result of your project!

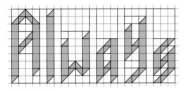

Example 1

This would be the arrangement using the master alphabet without modification. Kind of fun!

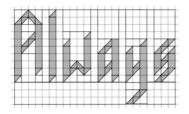

Example 2

I experimented with bringing down the 'y' sliding it down the scale, and adding 3-squares of grid height to the finished panel to compensate. This word is now 13-squares high.

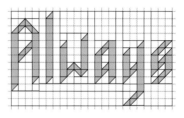

Example 3

The 'A' seemed a little too high. I slid it down along the grid aligning the HST of the 'A' and the 'l'. That looks better! Still 13-squares high.

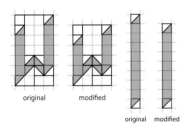

original   modified

original   modified

Modified Letters

Lastly, I modified the grid in the letters themselves to align the height of the 'w' and the 'l' by removing a grid-square from their height.

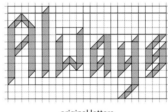

original letters
from master alphabet

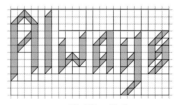

modified "l" and "w"

Side-by-Side Comparison

The total grid height of the panel on the right, my fully modified version, is now 12-squares. When looking at both versions side-by-side, the 'Always' on the right looks a bit more traditional to me and is slightly easier to read.

Once you have selected the word(s) you would like to piece, I really encourage you to photocopy the grid on page 12 and play around with sliding the grid or modifying the letters (or both!) in just the same way. See, I told you this was fun!

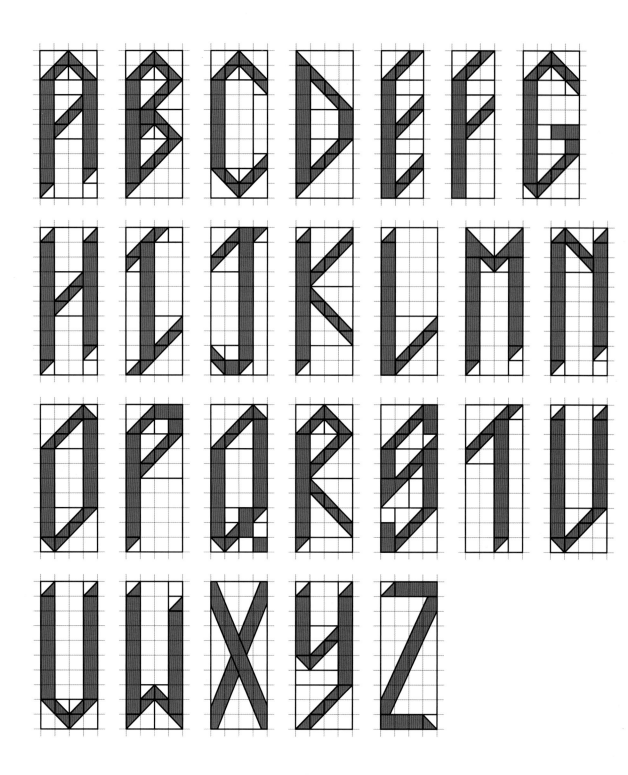

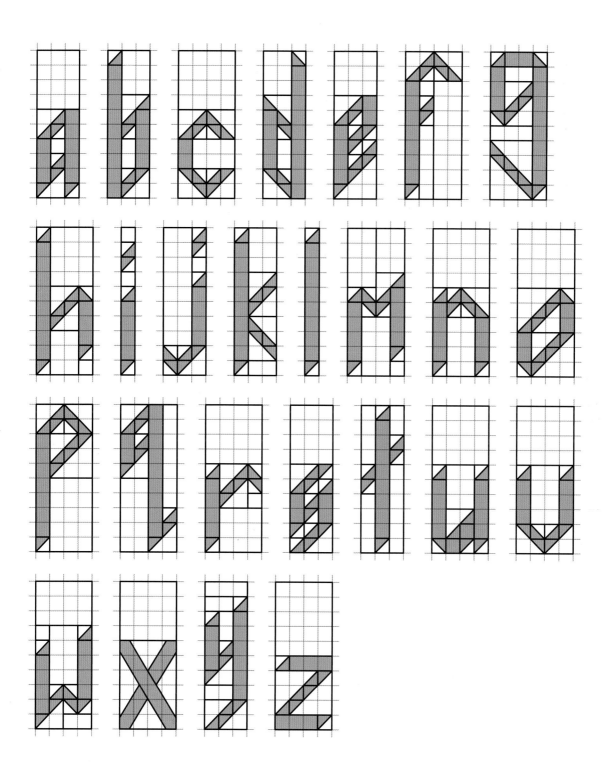

MAKE BANNER

Make something today! This banner will remind you to. It is made using the Spiky Alphabet. All the letters are pieced using a ½"-square grid size, or 1" cut. Remember to reference the master alphabet to create your word (see pages 40–41).

The banner is easy to customize. If you want to use a larger or longer word, simply piece each of the letters and decide how long you want your banner to be at the bottom. Use a single grid-square width of Background fabric between each letter and at the beginning and end of your word, to create your own Letter Panel. The width of your word will dictate the banner width, and your eye and preference will determine the corresponding height.

Finished Size: 9" x 14" but may vary depending on your word (23cm x 35.5cm)

MATERIALS

10" square of Main Fabric

7" (18cm) x WOF of Background Fabric

4" (10cm) x WOF of Letter Fabric

(1) 10" x 14" (25cm x 35cm) rectangle of Batting

(1) 10" x 14" (25cm x 35cm) rectangle of Backing Fabric

(1) 4" (10cm) x WOF of Sleeve Fabric

(1) 20" (50cm) length of ½" wide ribbon

Marking tool

Knitting needle, a dowel or similar support for hanging

CUTTING

From the Main Fabric, cut:
(1) 9½" x 7" rectangle
(1) 9½" x 2½" rectangle

From the Background Fabric, cut:
(1) 2⅜" x WOF strip, subcut into:

> (1) 2⅜" square subcut in half on the diagonal to create 1 triangle for the HSTs

> Trim the strip to 2" and subcut (2) 2" squares and (1) 2" x 1" rectangle

(1) 1⅞" x WOF strip, subcut into:

> (5) 1⅞" squares each subcut in half on the diagonal to create 9 triangles for HSTs (discard 1)

> Trim the strip to 1⅜" and cut (8) 1⅜" squares. Cut each in half on the diagonal to create 15 triangles

(1) 1½" x WOF strip, subcut into:

> (1) 1½" x 1" rectangle
> (1) 1½" x 2" rectangle
> (1) 1½" x 4" rectangle
> (2) 1" squares

(5) 1" x 5½" rectangles

From the Letter Fabric, cut:
(1) 1⅞" x WOF strip, subcut into:

> (1) 1⅞" square subcut in half on the diagonal to create 2 triangles for HSTs

> Trim the strip to 1⅜" and subcut (16) 1⅜" squares. Subcut these in half on the diagonal to create 32 triangles for the HSTs

(1) 1" x WOF strip, subcut into:
(1) 1" x 4½" rectangle
(1) 1" x 4" rectangle
(1) 1" x 3½" rectangle
(1) 1" x 3" rectangle
(1) 1" x 2½" rectangle
(1) 1" x 2" rectangle
(1) 1" x 1½" rectangle

From the Sleeve fabric, cut:
(1) 2½" x 10½" rectangle

Use a ¼" seam allowance unless otherwise noted.

ASSEMBLING THE LETTER PANEL

1 Using the Spiky Alphabet and a grid-square size of ½" (1" cut), piece the word 'M-a-k-e' (see pages 40–41). At this small size, some of the cut pieces are tiny! To help ensure accurate piecing, use an exact ¼" seam allowance and reduce the stitch length on your machine down a little, to a slightly smaller-than-normal stitch width.

> **TIP** When piecing with small cut units, go slowly, press carefully and you'll be just fine!

2 Using Figure 1 as a reference, add a 1-square grid width of Background fabric between each pieced letter and at the beginning and end of 'Make' (Fig. 1). With the right sides together, sew the columns together onto the Letter Panel and press the seams to one side. This finishes at 9½" wide and 5½" tall but of course yours may finish at a different size depending on the word you chose to feature. Press the Panel well.

Figure 1

ASSEMBLING THE BANNER

1 With the right sides facing, attach the 9½" x 2½" Main rectangle above the assembled Panel, and press towards the Main rectangle. Attach this 9½" x 7" rectangle below the assembled Letter Panel (Fig. 2). The Banner Front should measure 9½" x 14".

Figure 2

2 Mark a center point on the bottom raw edge of the assembled panel, 4¾" in from either side. Using the 45-degree line on your patchwork ruler, or a 45-degree triangle ruler, cut the bottom corners off the panel. Angle the cut at 45-degrees away from the center mark to make the point of the Banner. (Fig. 3)

4¾"   4¾"

Figure 3

3 Using the trimmed Banner Front from Step 2 as a template, cut the Batting and the Backing fabric to the same size and shape.

4 With the Backing fabric right side up, layer the Batting then the Banner Front face down on top of the stack. Pin through all three layers. Stitch around the edges of the Banner leaving the top edge open (Fig. 4). Trim the points close to the stitching at the corners and the bottom point of the Banner.

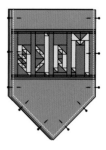

Figure 4

5 Turn the assembled unit from Step 4 right side out and use a knitting needle to push out the corners. Give the Banner a good press, making sure all the edges are sharp and tidy. Pin all around the edges again. Edgestitch around the perimeter of the Banner, leaving the top open. Topstitch across the two seams above and below the Letter Panel. Finally, baste the layers together along the top edge using a ⅛" seam allowance to secure the edges for the next step.

TIP *If you'd like to add any other quilting to your Banner, do so now before attaching the Sleeve.*

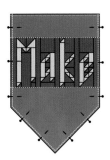

Figure 5

ATTACHING THE SLEEVE

1 Fold over the short ends of the Sleeve rectangle by ¼", wrong sides together and press. Fold again by ¼" and topstitch ⅛" from the outer edge. (Fig. 6)

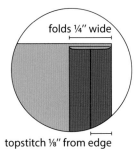

folds ¼" wide

topstitch ⅛" from edge

Figure 6

2 Press the Sleeve rectangle in half along the length. Open it up and position one raw edge along the top of the Banner, right sides together, with the Sleeve facing down towards the Banner. Stitch along the top edge of the Banner. (Fig. 7)

Figure 7

3 Press the remaining raw edge of the Sleeve over by ¼" to the wrong side of the fabric. Wrap the long folded edge over to the back of the Banner aligning the folded edge with the panel

of the Sleeve on the front. Pin in place. Stitch along the folded edge ⅛" from the fold through all the layers to secure the Sleeve. Finally, hand sew the edges of the Banner Sleeve together using a matching thread. Sew just at the ¼" seam so that the raw edges cannot be seen.

HANGING

To hang my Banner, I drilled two holes into a cute wooden knitting needle that had lost its partner. I slid the needle through the Sleeve, persuaded the ends of the ribbon to go through each hole and tied a knot to hold each end of the ribbon in place. If you don't have a drill, you can always tie the ribbon around a dowel to hang up your Banner. A little dot of craft glue stops the ribbon from sliding off the ends.

Depending on the diameter of the dowel, you might want to stitch another line ¼" up from the edge of the panel Sleeve seam for decorative purposes and to ensure a snug fit. I have done this for my knitting needle. If your hanging dowel is thicker than mine there may not be room. So, be sure to check first that you will have the space to fit in your dowel.

Hang the Banner from a doorknob or hook and enjoy your handiwork.

ALWAYS

As I am a mad Harry Potter fan, this quilt is a little nod to one of my favorite parts of the story. If you know what I'm talking about, your heart just melted—even if you don't, I'm sure you can appreciate the sentiment behind this sweet little cuddle quilt. How long will I love you? I will love you always.

This quilt is made using the Spiky Alphabet to piece the letters (see pages 40–41 and page 39 for modifications to the 'Always' panel). All the letters are pieced using a 1½"-square grid or a 2" cut size.

Finished Size: 51" x 63" (130cm x 160cm)

MATERIALS

3½ yards (3.2m) of Background Fabric

14" (35cm) x WOF of Letter Fabric

Scraps of various fabrics for Heart/Contrast Heart Blocks

15" (40cm) x WOF of Binding Fabric

4 yards (3.6m) of Backing Fabric

59" x 71" (150cm x 180cm) rectangle of Batting

Foundation piecing paper

Very fine, flat pins

Iron

New sewing machine needle

CUTTING

Cut the largest pieces first, then cut smaller pieces from the remaining strips. If you are using a directional print, you may need some additional fabric to match the orientation.

From the Background Fabric:
For the Heart Rows, cut:
(12) 5" x WOF strips, subcut into:
  (1) 42½" x 5" rectangle
  (2) 36½" x 5" rectangles
  (2) 35" x 5" rectangles
  (1) 30½" x 5" rectangle
  (1) 29" x 5" rectangle
  (2) 27½" x 5" rectangles
  (1) 24½" x 5" rectangle
  (1) 23" x 5" rectangle
  (2) 20" x 5" rectangles
  (1) 18½" x 5" rectangle
  (1) 17" x 5" rectangle
  (2) 12½" x 5" rectangles
  (2) 11" x 5" rectangles
  (1) 5" square

For the Always Panel/Row, cut:
(1) 6½" x 18½" rectangle

(6) 3⅞" squares. Subcut each along the diagonal into 12 triangles for the large HSTs

(13) 2⅜" squares. Subcut each along the diagonal into 26 triangles for the small HSTs

(2) 3½" x WOF strips, subcut into:
  (1) 3½" x 26" rectangle
  (1) 3½" x 18½" rectangle
  (1) 3½" x 6½" rectangle
  (1) 3½" x 5" rectangle
  (4) 3½" x 2" rectangles

(3) 2" x WOF strips, subcut into:
  (5) 2" x 14" rectangles
  (2) 2" x 18½" rectangles
  (1) 2" x 15½" rectangle
  (3) 2" squares

(1) 5" x WOF strip, subcut into:
  (1) 5" x 14" rectangle
  (2) 5" x 6½" rectangles
  (3) 5" squares

For the Heart Blocks, cut:
(22) 5½" x 3" rectangles for pieces A2 and A3

(5) 2½" x WOF strips, subcut into:
  (22) 2½" x 3½" rectangles for B1 and C1
  (11) 2½" x 3" rectangles for C3
  (22) 2½" squares for B3 and C4

From the Letter Fabric, cut:
(2) 2⅜" x WOF strips, subcut into:
  (25) 2⅜" squares. Subcut each along the diagonal into 50 triangles for the small HSTs (discard 1)

(2) 2" x WOF strips, subcut into:
  (2) 2" x 10½" rectangles
  (2) 2" x 9" rectangles
  (1) 2" x 8" rectangle
  (4) 2" x 5" rectangles
  (1) 2" x 3½" rectangle

From the Heart Fabrics, cut:
  (10) 4" squares for A1

  (20) 2½" squares for B2 and C2

From the Contrast Heart Fabric(s), cut:
  (1) 4" square for A1

  (2) 2½" squares for B2 and C2

From the Binding Fabric, cut:
  (6) 2½" x WOF strips

From the 45"-wide Backing Fabric (if using), cut:
  (2) 72" x WOF lengths (see page 109 for assembly).

Use a ¼" seam allowance unless otherwise noted.

TIP *Change the needle in your machine. I always keep a machine needle that is just for foundation paper piecing—the paper blunts them and then they aren't good for fabric. Or use the one that's in there already and throw it away afterwards. Did you know sewing machine needles should be replaced after every 12 hours of stitching? Come on, own up—how old IS that thing??*

PAPER PIECING THE HEART BLOCKS

1 Make 11 copies of the heart foundation patterns (see page 121) onto your preferred paper for paper piecing.

TIP *Foundation paper has a looser texture than copy paper, will tear away more easily after being stitched and is easier for your machine to sew through. The result is less machine wear and neat, smooth stitches.*

2 Adjust the stitch length on your sewing machine to about 1.8 or lower, and set your iron to a medium setting, with no steam.

3 Use your favorite method to foundation piece each of the three sections.

JOINING THE SECTIONS

1 When all the sections are pieced, trim them to the correct size (including the grey seam allowance).

2 To attach the sections, align the blue // marks and the raw edges on Section A and Section B with the right sides facing and sew. Tear away any paper covering the seam allowances and press the seam open. Repeat to sew Section C to the A/B Section. (Fig. 1)

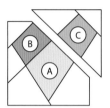

Figure 1

3 Press well and repeat for all 11 hearts, checking that each is trimmed to 5" square and carefully removing all the papers once assembled.

ASSEMBLING THE ALWAYS PANEL

1 Using the 1½" (2" cut) grid for each square measurement, sew the letters 'A-l-w-a-y-s' using the Letter and Background fabrics. Refer to the Spiky Alphabet (see pages 40–41) and my modified 'Always' panel (see page 39) for general piecing instructions. Refer to the Assembly Diagram for additional Background cutting sizes and placements.

2 Add the remaining Background pieces to and around the pieced letters and join together into a Panel.

ASSEMBLING THE QUILT TOP

1 With the right sides facing, sew the 20½" x 5" and 27½" x 5" Background rectangles together along the short ends to make a 47" long rectangle.

2 Use the Assembly Diagram on the facing page as a reference for placement. Arrange the Background rectangles, Always panel, and heart blocks in 10 rows on a flat surface or a design wall if you have one.

3 Refer to Adding Borders or Long Strips (see page 108), for tips on joining the strips together. Piece the segments in each of the 10 rows.

4 Sew the rows together pressing the seams in alternate directions as you progress. Give the entire top a good press when the piecing is complete.

FINISHING

Layer the Backing rectangle with the wrong side up, then the Batting, and finally the quilt top right side up. Baste, quilt, and attach the binding using your favorite method.

QUILTING

The ALWAYS quilt was machine quilted by Kat Jones. Kat used white thread and echo stitched around the heart shapes in the white background. She then filled in the negative space with straight vertical lines ½" apart.

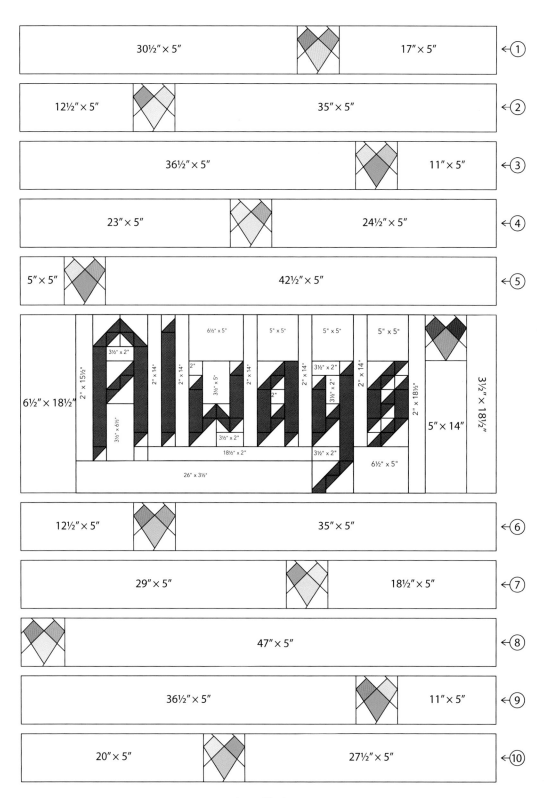

30½" × 5"	17" × 5"	← ①
12½" × 5"	35" × 5"	← ②
36½" × 5"	11" × 5"	← ③
23" × 5"	24½" × 5"	← ④
5" × 5"	42½" × 5"	← ⑤

6½" × 18½"

2" × 15½"
3½" × 2"
2" × 14"
2" × 14"
2"
3½" × 5"
6½" × 5"
5" × 5"
5" × 5"
5" × 5"
2" × 14"
2"
2" × 14"
3½" × 2"
2" × 14"
3½" × 2"
3½" × 2"
2" × 18½"
5" × 14"
3½" × 18½"
3½" × 6½"
3½" × 2"
18½" × 2"
3½" × 2"
26" × 3½"
6½" × 5"

| 12½" × 5" | 35" × 5" | ← ⑥
| 29" × 5" | 18½" × 5" | ← ⑦
| 47" × 5" | | ← ⑧
| 36½" × 5" | 11" × 5" | ← ⑨
| 20" × 5" | 27½" × 5" | ← ⑩

Assembly Diagram

THE

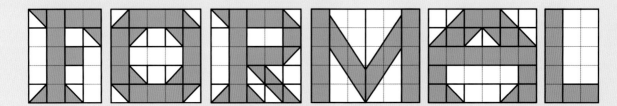

ALPHABET

The Formal Alphabet is nice and blocky. I love using it for high-impact single-word row quilts like FREEDOM and the SLEEPY quilt on the right because the letters finish in a variety of widths unlike some of our other alphabets. Though there isn't a pattern for the SLEEPY quilt included here, it is easy to see that this is a simple scrappy approach using a variety of Letter and Background fabrics to make letters using a 2" square grid. Then to finish off, I added a top and bottom border in grey letters to match the single letter 'S's and 'Y's that I used as side borders.

LET'S PRACTICE!

THE FORMAL ALPHABET

This alphabet is a bit more formal than the others. It has a lot of structure like our Chubby Alphabet, is traditionally pieced and works on a grid 5-squares high, with varying widths. This allows for easy size adjustments to suit your project. Our Formal Alphabet uses a lot of HSTs to provide those attractive angles.

As with our other alphabets, there is an instruction grid (see pages 56–57) for all the letters in the alphabet. While most of the letters are made up of squares, rectangles and HSTs, some uppercase letters use customized, inset letter fabric pieces. These include the uppercase 'M' and 'V'.

THE LETTER F

1 Let's start by making the letter 'F'. This time, we will be creating an 8" x 10" finished block so we are using a 2" grid. (Fig. 1)

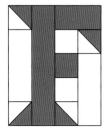

Figure 1

2 Using 3½" squares from each of the Background and Letter fabrics, make (4) 2½" Background/Letter HST units (see page 11).

3 The 'F' is assembled in columns. From the Background fabric, cut (1) 2½" x 8½" rectangle, (1) 2½" x 6½" rectangle, and (2) 2½" squares. From the Letter fabric, cut (1) 2½" x 10½" rectangle, (1) 4½" x 2½" rectangle and (1) 2½" square. Using Figure 2 as a reference, arrange all of the units as shown.

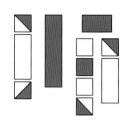

Figure 2

4 Attach an HST to either end of the large Background rectangle, then assemble the (4) 2½" squares into a column and the smaller Background rectangle and remaining HST into another column.

5 Next sew together along their length, the assembled columns from Step 4. Be careful to match the points as you go (Fig. 3). Press.

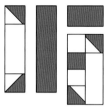

Figure 3

Modified Angle Assembly Diagram

THE MODIFIED 'F' FOR THE FREEDOM QUILT

In order to replicate the look of the original inspiration font used by Jessie B. Telfair (see page 59), I modified the 'F' slightly. It's much easier to piece using an HST as in the master alphabet, but if you would like to piece it as I did, here is what you need to know.

1 Begin by replacing the second Letter square on the top of the 'F' with a 2½" strip square of Letter/Background fabric. Sew together (1) 1½" x 2½" rectangle of each fabric to form a 2½" strip square. (Fig. 4)

Figure 4

2 Next, we are creating a smaller angle for the top right of the 'F'. To do this, take a 2½" square of Letter fabric and, on the wrong side, make a mark halfway up the right side (in this case at 1¼"). The rest of the measurements are the seam allowances and will be consistent for any size you are making. Mark a dot 1¼" high and ¼" away from the raw edge. Make a second dot ¼" in from the bottom and left sides. Draw a straight line to connect these two dots. (Fig. 5)

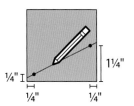

Figure 5

3 Referencing the Modified Angle Assembly Diagram above, trim the Letter square ¼" away from the drawn line. With the right sides together, layer a 3" x 2" Background rectangle on top, aligning the raw edges as shown. Stitch on the drawn line. Open up and press. Trim the unit to 2½" square.

4 Finally, replace the far right Letter/Background fabric HST with a 2½" square of Background fabric.

The modified 'F'!

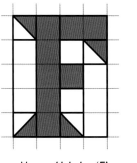 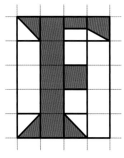

Master Alphabet 'F' *Modified 'F'*

INSET STRIP LETTERS

The 'M', 'W', 'N' and 'V' are made slightly differently. Instead of working with a set of HSTs to create the smaller angles that most of the blocks in this alphabet use, we will use inset Letter fabric on the diagonal to achieve the sharp angles.

Let's work on the letter 'M' as an example, using the same 10" finished height and the 2" square grid used in the FREEDOM quilt (see page 60).

1 Cut two Background rectangles measuring half the width of your finished block plus the ½" seam allowance and the same height as the unfinished block. In this case, cut (2) 5½" x 11½" rectangles of the Background fabric. Measure and mark half the finished width of the rectangle (in this instance, 1½") up from the bottom right hand corner. Repeat on the bottom left hand corner of the other rectangle. (Fig. 6)

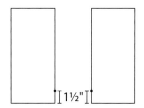

Figure 6

2 On one Background rectangle, cut from the top left-hand corner to the 1½" mark from Step 1. Repeat with the second rectangle cutting from the top right-hand corner to the 1½" mark from Step 1. (Fig. 7)

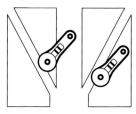

Figure 7

3 Cut two strips of Letter fabric. Make these 1-square grid wide plus ½" for seam allowances and long enough to extend beyond the Background rectangle on both ends (in this instance the strips should be 2½" wide by about 14" long).

4 Center the Letter strip between both halves of a subcut Background rectangle from Step 2. Both short edges of the Letter Strip will extend past the Background rectangle. With the right sides facing, attach the strip to one half of the subcut Background rectangle. Press. Repeat to attach the second half of the subcut Background rectangle to the other long raw edge of the Letter strip. Press.

5 Repeat Step 4 with the remaining subcut Background rectangle and Letter strip. (Fig. 8)

Figure 8

6 On the left assembled unit from Figure 8, mark a point on the lower inside corner ¼" away from the edges on the seam of the Letter strip and Background triangle. Trim ¼" away from this mark along the bottom and inside. Finally, trim the unit to 4½" x 10½", the same height as the unfinished block and the width of a third of the finished block + ½" for seam allowances.

7 Repeat for the remaining unit from Figure 8. (Fig. 9)

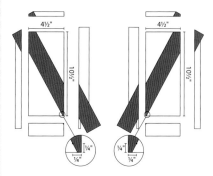

Figure 9

8 Cut two rectangles of Letter fabric the same width as in Step 3 and the same height as the unfinished block. Arrange into four columns. (Fig. 10)

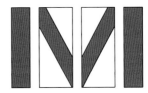

Figure 10

9 Sew the four columns along their long sides and press. This will be a 10½" unfinished block. (Fig. 11)

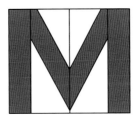

Figure 11

10 The 'W' is exactly the same block as a we made for the 'M', only it is inverted when completed. (Fig. 12)

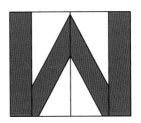

Figure 12

The letters 'N' and 'V' are constructed using the same inset technique.

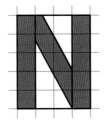

Figure 13

1 To make the 'N' (Fig. 13), cut one Background rectangle of fabric half the width of your finished block plus the ½" seam allowance. In this case, a 4½" x 10½" rectangle. Measure and mark half the finished width of the rectangle (in this instance, 1½") up from the bottom right hand corner. Cut from the bottom right mark up to the top left hand corner as in Figure 7 on the facing page.

2 Cut a strip of letter fabric the width of 1-grid square plus ½" for seam allowances, and long enough to extend beyond the background rectangle on both ends (in our case, 2½" x 14"). Center and sew the strip between the two halves of the Background triangles from Step 1, then follow the instructions on the facing page from Step 6 onward. This letter will be an 8½" x 10½" unfinished block.

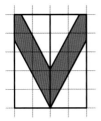

Figure 14

1 To make the 'V' (Fig. 14), follow the instructions in Step 1 for making the 'N', but this time make two units: one right leaning and one left leaning. Trim each piece back to half the width of your finished block plus the ½" seam allowance. In this case, a 4½" x 10½" rectangle. Press.

2 Stitch the two halves together up the center seam to create the letter 'V', taking care to match the points of the 'V' at the bottom. This letter will be an 8½" x 10½" unfinished block.

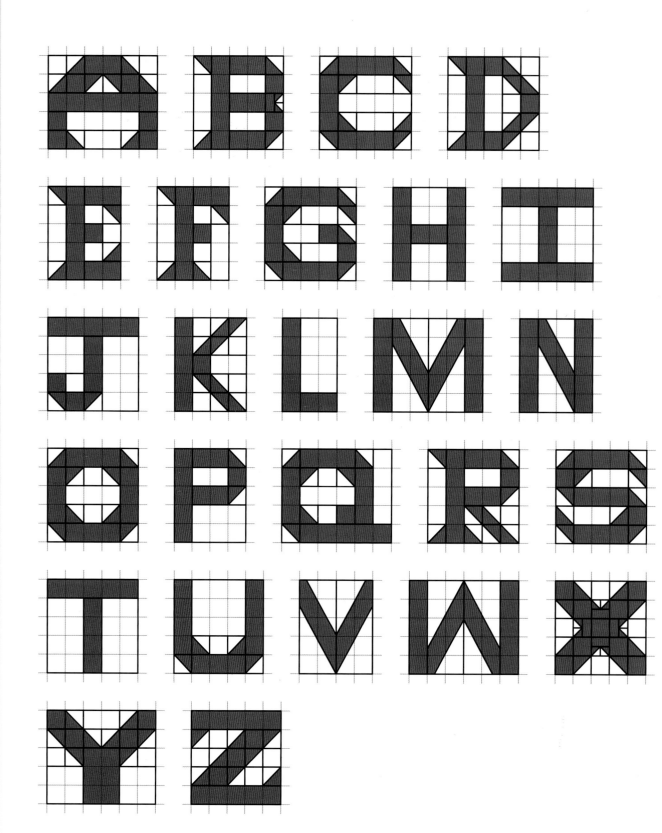

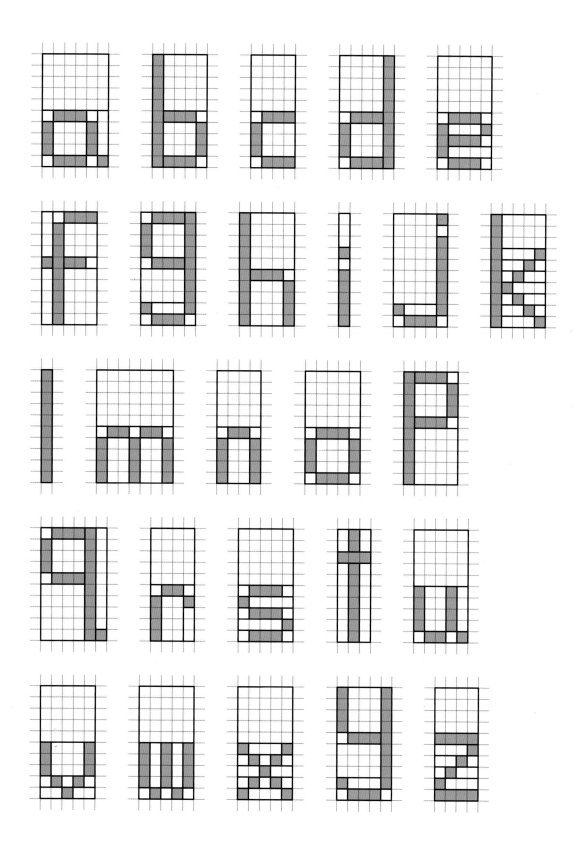

FREEDOM

The use of text in quilts is not a modern phenomenon —in fact text quilts have an important place in quilt history. From very early quilts, historians have been able to find many examples of words quilted into fabrics, pieced or appliquéd letters, or signatures on blocks.

For this alphabet, I have used a wonderful vintage quilt (see facing page) made by Jessie B. Telfair as the source of inspiration for my quilt pattern. This quilt, Freedom, is an African American quilt from the rural South of the United States.

An emphasis on bright solid fabrics in the colors of the American flag, a bold, repetitive graphic design, asymmetry and strong contrast are what makes this quilt sing. While freedom quilts can be traced back to the US Civil War, this quilt is relatively new. It was made by Jessie B. Telfair in 1983, and is one of forty three quilts that the artist created using a similar design. Telfair made the quilts in a series, to capture her feelings of anger when she lost her job in a school kitchen after she tried to register to vote in the 1960's.

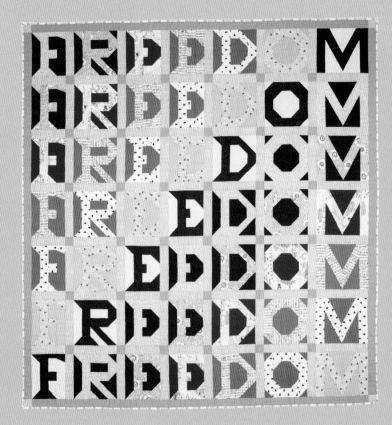

The repetition of the word FREEDOM captures the frustration and bitterness of the message in this piece. The important history and strong feelings behind this quilt moved me to use it as an example of historical text in this book. As much as we all love our patchworking, quilts aren't always about being light hearted, celebrating a holiday, or making something pretty. Quilts have always been an expression of the person who created them. Sometimes the text in quilts says things we may not want to hear. Your quilts are your voice, use them to say what matters to you.

The idea of Telfair's quilt really captured my imagination. Freedom may not mean the same to everyone, but in the world we are living in, it seems that freedom becomes more precious every day. To a quilter? Perhaps freedom from obligations so we have time to stitch; freedom to make what we like; freedom to use our own colors or design our own blocks—or freedom to shop for new fabric without guilt!

You can vary the background colors as I did to reinforce the horizontal and diagonal of each word, or just use a single background fabric for a subtler effect.

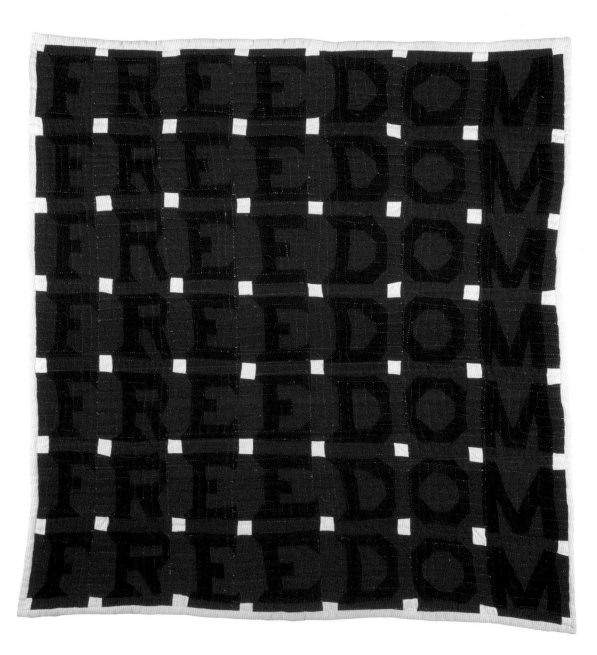

The original quilt made by Jessie B. Telfair in 1983 and gifted to the American Folk Art Museum after her death by her sister, Judith Alexander in loving memory. The photograph is by Gavin Ashworth and reprinted by permission of the American Folk Art Museum/ Art Resources, NY.

Finished quilt size: 82" x 86" (208cm x 218cm)

MATERIALS

²⁄₃ yard (60cm) each of seven shades for the Background

⁵⁄₈ yard (50cm) each of seven different prints for the Letters

1⁵⁄₈ yards (1.5m) for the Sashing

⁷⁄₈ yard (80cm) for the Cornerstones

¾ yard (70cm) for the Binding

7⁵⁄₈ yards (7m) for the Backing

90" x 94" (2.3m x 2.4m) rectangle of Batting

CUTTING

For the Letter 'F'
From each of the seven Background Fabrics, cut:
- (1) 2½" x 8½" rectangle
- (1) 2½" x 4½" rectangle
- (1) 2½" x 1½" rectangle
- (2) 2½" squares
- (2) 2⅞" squares, cut once diagonally

From each of the seven Letter Fabrics, cut:
- (1) 2½" x 10½" rectangle
- (1) 4½" x 2½" rectangle
- (1) 2½" square
- (2) 2⅞" squares, cut once diagonally

NOTE *For the 'F' in my quilt, I decided to piece a slightly trickier modified 'F' (see page 53) to replicate Jessie's quilt more closely. Use either version!*

For the Letter 'R'
From each of the seven Background Fabrics, cut:
- (1) 2½" x 6½" rectangle
- (1) 4½" x 2½" rectangle
- (1) 2½" square
- (5) 2⅞" squares, cut once diagonally

From each of the seven Letter Fabrics, cut:
- (1) 2½" x 10½" rectangle
- (2) 4½" x 2½" rectangles
- (1) 2½" square
- (5) 2⅞" squares, cut once diagonally

For the Letter 'E'
From each of the seven Background Fabrics, cut:
- (2) 2½" x 6½" rectangles
- (3) 2½" squares
- (2) 2⅞" squares, cut once diagonally

From each of the seven Letter Fabrics, cut:
- (1) 2½" x 10½" rectangle
- (1) 2½" square
- (2) 4½" x 2½" rectangles
- (2) 2⅞" squares, cut once diagonally

For the Letter 'D'
From each of the seven Background Fabrics, cut:
- (2) 2½" x 6½" rectangles
- (3) 2½" squares
- (4) 2⅞" squares, cut once diagonally

From each of the seven Letter Fabrics, cut:
- (1) 2½" x 10½" rectangle
- (3) 2½" squares
- (4) 2⅞" squares, cut once diagonally

For the Letter 'O'
From each of the seven Background Fabrics, cut:
- (1) 2½" x 6½" rectangle
- (2) 2½" squares
- (4) 2⅞" squares, cut once diagonally

From each of the seven Letter Fabrics, cut:
- (4) 2½" x 6½" rectangles (2 vertical, 2 horizontal)
- (4) 2⅞" squares, cut once diagonally

For the Letter 'M'
From each of the seven Background Fabrics, cut:
- (2) 5½" x 10½" rectangles

From each of the seven Letter Fabrics, cut:
- (2) 2½" x 10½" rectangles
- (2) 2½" x 14" rectangles

From the Sashing Fabric, cut:
- (22) 2½" x WOF strips. Subcut into:
  - (6) 2½" x 12½" rectangles
  - (60) 2½" x 10½" rectangles
  - (18) 2½" x 8½" rectangles
  - (4) 2½" squares for border

From the Cornerstone Fabric, cut:
- (11) 2½" x WOF strips. Subcut 3 of the strips into:
  - (36) 2½" squares
  - Save the remainder for the border.

From the Binding Fabric, cut:
- (9) 3" x WOF strips

Use a ¼" seam allowance unless otherwise noted.

CONSTRUCTING THE LETTERS

Referencing the alphabet grids on page 56, piece together seven 'F', 'R', 'D', 'O' and 'M's (1 in each color combination) and 14 'E's (2 in each color combination). Each 'F' and 'E' block will finish at 8½" wide. Each 'R', 'D', and 'O' will finish at 10½" square, and the 'M' blocks will be 12½" wide.

ASSEMBLING THE QUILT TOP

1 Referencing the Assembly Diagram, arrange the blocks into seven rows spelling out 'FREEDOM' with the colors running diagonally across the quilt. Place a 2½" x 10½" vertical sashing strip between each block.

2 Sew the blocks together into rows, pressing the seams towards the Sashing strips.

3 Make six Sashing rows, with a Cornerstone square in between each strip. Take care to match the width of the strip to the width of the corresponding letter. Each row will need seven Sashing strips in the following order:
8½", Cornerstone, 10½", Cornerstone, 8½", Cornerstone, 8½", Cornerstone, 10½", Cornerstone, 10½", Cornerstone, 12½"

4 Stitch the rows together with a Sashing/Cornerstone row in between each. Press all the seams towards the Sashing.

5 Sew all the remaining Cornerstone strips together into one long strip (see page 108 for Adding Borders). Measure and cut (2) 86½" long strips, and sew them to the sides of the quilt. Press towards the Border.

6 Trim the remaining Cornerstone strip to (2) 82½" strips. Add Sashing squares to each end. Sew to the top and bottom of the quilt. Press towards the Border.

FINISHING

Layer the Backing rectangle with the wrong side up, then the Batting, and finally the quilt top right side up. Baste, quilt, and attach the binding using your favorite method.

QUILTING

The quilting was done by Jayne Rennie in a wavy linear pattern, to reinforce the idea of a flag waving in the breeze. This quilting design also adds a subtle texture without competing with the blocky style of the Formal alphabet.

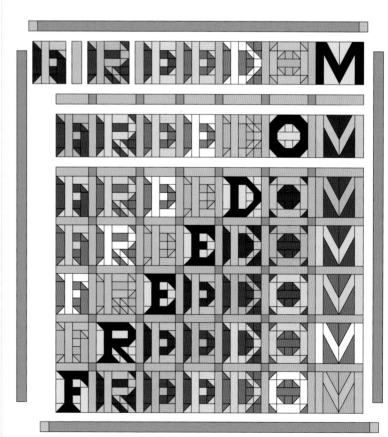

Assembly Diagram

4

THE
Back to Black
ALPHABET

LET'S PRACTICE!
BACK TO BLACK

In this section, we will be moving on from the square and straight alphabets to the free-flowing and elegant ones of the Back to Black Alphabet. This is based on the font created by Misti Hammers. The letters are intended for hand appliqué, but you could also use these templates for machine appliqué. My favorite method is hand needleturn appliqué, and so I have provided instructions for using my method on page 112–114. Remember that if you are using the templates to make fusible machine appliqué, they must be traced onto a fusible in reverse so that the letters read correctly after they are pressed onto the wrong side of the Letter fabric, cut out and turned right side up.

Back to Black includes a complete alphabet of uppercase and lowercase cursive letters (see pullout), but once you practice joining the letters together to form completely attached words, you can try using any script font you like (just be sure you are compliant with licensing and permissions!). Once you learn how to join the letters, the world is your oyster. I do recommend selecting a font that isn't too complicated with many flourishes or lots of tiny thin lines. Our font is fairly complex with its curly ends, so the stitching can be quite challenging.

TIP *If you have never tried needleturn appliqué before, consider omitting the curls on the patterns provided. Instead, just try rounding the ends of your letters.*

Once you have decided on the letter or word you are going to stitch, you will need to make the pattern for your cursive words from the letters provided in the pullout. The first and most important step is to learn how to join the letters together to form a cursive word.

Depending on how large or long your word is, you may need a few pieces of paper taped together on which to trace your word. If there is a natural break in the word, divide it into two or more patterns that you may still be able to fit on one piece of paper. We are going to practice with the word 'w-o-r-r-y'.

CREATING A PATTERN

1 Using a piece of regular paper and a pencil, draw a straight horizontal line about ⅓ of the way up from the bottom of the sheet. Next, add a few orientation lines. These are vertical lines that will help keep the letters straight. I recommend drawing one at the halfway mark and two others near the quarter distances across the paper. (Fig. 1)

Figure 1

2 Using a well-lit window, a light box or a glass table with a lamp under it, trace the letter at the beginning of the word onto the horizontal line of the grid from Step 1. The Back to Black letters are slanted italics, so as you progress use the lines from Step 1 to help keep the letters on the same level and at the correct angle to each other. (Fig. 2)

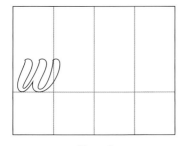

Figure 2

3 Measure ¼" to the right of the outermost edge of the first letter and trace the second letter. Don't worry about joining the letters yet.

4 Repeat Step 3 to trace the entire word(s) using multiple pattern sheets if necessary.

JOINING

All the letters in this alphabet have a lovely, cursive tail on them. You will find that for the most part they will butt up to each other very nicely. For example, to spell the word 'worry', the 'o' 'r' 'r' and 'y' would all join up and space apart beautifully using their existing tails. (Fig. 3)

Figure 3

The 'o' joins nicely with the two 'r's also. (Fig. 4)

Figure 4

There are a few lowercase letters in the alphabet that don't have the tail for you to make a join. As with most alphabets in this book, Back to Black is customizable so you will have a 'joining up' decision to make.

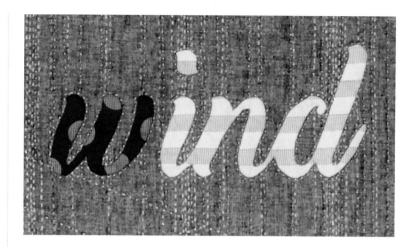

In my WINDSWEPT quilt detail above, I opted to leave the letter 'w' sitting out in front of the word 'wind'. The lowercase 'w' doesn't have a natural join in the Back to Black font, so I could have drafted my pattern either with or without a join between the 'w' and the 'i-n-d'

If you have a situation where you really feel the letters need joining, simply sketch in a slightly curving bar to connect the pieces. Below you can see what our example word 'worry' would look like with and without a join. (Fig. 5)

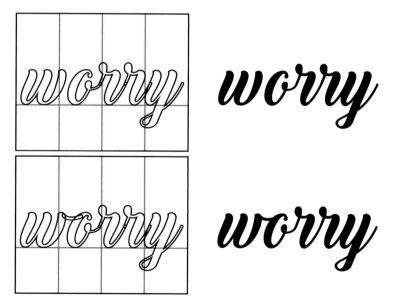

Figure 5

STITCH

There are times every now and then when the combinations of letters you have won't join or sit together perfectly. The perfect example of this is on the front cover of the book! The cross bars on the letter 't' didn't sit nicely against each other, and right where they were going to cross over, the dot on the 'i' would have been hidden. To fix the problem, I sketched the 't' bar as one long bar instead of two separate ones, and moved the dot over the 'i' up a little so it floated above (Fig. 6). Any time you have a problem with letters clashing, you can always shift them apart a little and sketch the piece joining them to be a little longer, or change their shapes slightly to accommodate each other.

Figure 6

When you have drawn your words on paper and joined the letters together, as you would like them to be in your appliqué, you are ready to make templates.

MAKING TEMPLATES

There are a few different ways to create the templates for tracing. Here are some of my favorite methods.

LAMINATING MACHINE

My favorite way of creating durable templates is by feeding the drawn patterns through a laminating machine. These are relatively inexpensive to purchase, especially if you are planning to create a lot of words to appliqué to your quilt top. Alternately, research whether your local copy or quilt shop has one available to rent. Once laminated, the templates can be easily and accurately cut using a pair of sharp scissors and will have a nice firm edges that hold their shape when traced around on the appliqué fabric.

TRACING

Transfer your word to a piece of cardboard or template plastic. Because our Back to Black font has so many little curves and curls, I don't recommend using regular paper on which to create the template. This paper is just too flimsy and you will have trouble keeping an accurate shape. Making a cardboard template for needleturn appliqué results in a nice sharp, smooth stitching line.

LIGHT BOX

If you have a large enough one (or your word is small enough!), you can use a light box to trace the pattern directly onto fabric if preferred.

Whichever template-making method you use, cut out the letters that are joined together as one whole template. For example, if you didn't connect the 'w' to the rest of the word in our practice pattern, the 'o-r-r-y' will be cut from a single template material, and the 'w' will be cut from another.

CUTTING THE APPLIQUÉ

Trace around the outer perimeter of the template(s) onto the right side of the appliqué fabric, using a silver gel pen (see page 112 for more detail regarding why and how to use these in appliqué). Cut around only the outer perimeter of the transferred template line using a scant ¼" seam allowance at this point. (Fig. 7)

Figure 7

TIP *If you now cut away all the little curves and holes in the letters, the appliqué transforms into a tangle of fabric spaghetti and is incredibly difficult to place onto the background fabric—ask me how I know!*

ALIGNING THE APPLIQUÉ

1 To assist in aligning the appliqué onto the background fabric in smaller projects, fold the background fabric into quarters and finger press a crease along both folds. If the piece is larger, usually instruction is given in the pattern for placement measurement, but if you are creating your own pattern, follow my method.

2 Using the creases from Step 1 as a guide, center and align the words or simply use them to assist in maintaining horizontal alignment.

3 Once you are happy with the orientation of the appliqué on the background fabric, you are ready to attach it temporarily. To do this, apply a tiny dab of liquid appliqué glue to the wrong side of your fabric appliqué. Be sure not to get any of the glue within ¼" of the gel pen line to allow the seam allowance to be tucked under. Use tiny dots of liquid appliqué glue in the larger sections of the letters, to secure the appliqué to the background fabric. Use tacking stitches where needed in the thinner sections so that there is space to turn the fabric under without the glue getting in the way. Again, only a few TINY dots of glue on each shape are needed to secure them in place.

TIP *I use liquid appliqué glue to temporarily fix the appliqué onto a background fabric. This ensures that my project is easily transportable, and lets me curl the fabric up in my hand as I stitch so I can avoid being stuck by a sharp pin. The glue washes out and the attached appliqué can be ironed once it is dry.*

4 Let the glue dry for a few minutes and you are ready to use your favorite method of appliqué to attach the word(s) to the background fabric. If you'd like to use my needleturn method, see page 112–114 for easy to follow instructions.

MONOGRAM SHOPPER

This bag is just the right size to fit in some groceries and that bunch of sunflowers you bought for the kitchen bench. It holds lots of craft supplies for a sew day too!

This bag would make a lovely gift for a friend or a swap partner, personalized with their initial. It's quick to make and a great use for all those linen and canvas prints on the market that are so tempting to buy!

Finished size: 19½" high x 10" wide x 8" deep (50 cm x 25cm x 20cm)

MATERIALS

⅔ yard (60cm) x 45" or wider WOF canvas/linen or ⅞ yard (80cm) if using quilting cotton for Exterior and Handles

⅞ yard (80cm) x WOF for the Lining and Handle Lining

2" x WOF for the Contrast strip

6" x 12" rectangles each of 5 different fabrics for the Blades

8"–11" square for the Circle (see the Note)

8"–11" square for the Monogram

Silver gel pen

50 or 80 weight cotton thread to match appliqué fabrics

Template plastic or similar

Milliners needles

Liquid appliqué glue

CUTTING

From the Template Plastic, cut:
   1 Blade and one Circle from the patterns on page 127

   1 Back to Black Alphabet Letter on the pullout

From the Blade Fabrics, cut:
   4 Blades from each rectangle, for a total of 20 Blades

From the Monogram Fabric, cut:
   1 Back to Black letter

From the Exterior Fabric, cut:
   (2) 19" x 23" rectangles

   (2) 2" x 23" rectangles for the Handles

From the Lining Fabric, cut:
   (2) 19" x 24" rectangles

   (2) 2" x 23" rectangles for the Handle Lining

From the Contrast Fabric, cut:
   (2) 19" x 1½" strips

NOTE *There are three sizes for the center Circle, as some of the letters are larger than the others.*

MAKING THE PLATE

1 Trim the Blade template by ¼" along the turning line (Fig. 1). Use the trimmed template and the gel pen to transfer the turning line onto the right side of each of the 20 Blades.

Figure 1

2 The plate is stitched together in four quarters. Each quarter contains one Blade of each fabric color, repeated in the same order.

> **TIP** *I recommend arranging the blades in order on a flat surface before stitching.*

3 Position two Blades right sides together. It is important to use an accurate ¼" seam so that the assembled Plate lies flat. Starting at the narrower end, stitch towards the wider end, finishing at the marked line from Step 1. Staystitch or backstitch where you finish stitching. (Fig. 2)

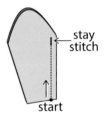

Figure 2

4 Repeat Step 3 to attach five Blades forming a quarter circle with 90-degree straight edges. Repeat to make four Plate quarters. Press the seams to one side. (Fig. 3)

Figure 3

5 Stitch together two pairs of plate quarters into two plate halves, then join the halves together to make the Plate. There will be a hole at the center and the plate should lie flat. If your plate is too small, you will need to undo some seams to make them a bit more scant, and if it is too large you can always pleat the seams a little at the narrow end a little as the Circle will cover them. (Fig. 4)

Figure 4

ASSEMBLING THE FRONT

1 Using the gel pen, trace the Circle Pattern in your chosen size onto the right side of the Circle square, but do not cut yet.

2 Center the Monogram within the drawn circle from Step 1 and use your favorite appliqué method to secure.

3 Cut around the Circle using a scant ¼" seam allowance outside the pen line. (Fig. 5)

Figure 5

4 Fold the Circle into quarters and finger press to form creases (Fig. 6). Fold a 19" x 23" Exterior rectangle in half along the width and 9½" away from the top short edge. Press to form creases. (Fig. 7)

Figure 6

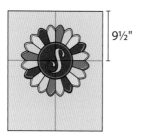

9½"

Figure 7

5 Use the creases in the Circle and the seams of the Plate to layer them onto the Exterior rectangle. Glue in place using liquid appliqué glue.

6 Finger press along the turning line of the plate blades, and then use your favorite appliqué method to stitch the Plate and the Circle to form the assembled Exterior Front panel.

ASSEMBLING AND ATTACHING THE HANDLES

1 Position a 2" x 23" Exterior rectangle and Lining rectangle right sides together. Stitch along both long edges to make a tube, and then push the tube right sides out using a knitting needle or chopstick. Press the handle flat. Edgestitch along each of the long edges. (Fig. 8)

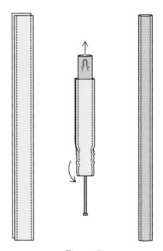

Figure 8

2 Repeat Step 1 with the remaining 2" x 23" Exterior and Lining rectangles.

3 With the right side of the Exterior Front panel facing up and aligning the raw edges, position both short ends of an assembled Handle (with the Lining facing up) along the top 19" edge. Each outer edge of the Handle should be 4" away from the sides of the Panel. Ensure that the Handle is not twisted. Pin and baste in place using a ⅛" seam allowance. (Fig. 9)

Figure 9

4 With the right sides together, pin a 19" x 1½" Contrast strip to the top of the assembled unit from Step 3, covering the Handle. Stitch using a ¼" seam allowance and press the Contrast strip up and all the seam allowances down towards the Exterior so the raw edges of the Handle are against the wrong side of the Exterior Front panel. (Fig. 10)

Figure 10

5 Topstitch just inside the seam of the Contrast strip. This will prevent the Handle from flipping up while adding a nice finishing touch. (Fig. 11)

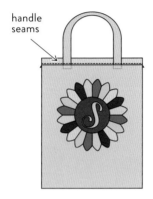

handle seams

Figure 11

6 Repeat Steps 3–5 with the remaining Exterior rectangle, Handle and Contrast strip.

BOXING THE CORNERS

1 Position the assembled Exterior panels right sides together, aligning the raw edges and the seams on the Contrast strip. Be sure the Handles are neatly tucked inside, away from the sides. Using a sharp pencil, draw a 4" square onto both the bottom corners. Use scissors or a rotary cutter to cut these squares away through both layers of the bag. Pin or clip in place and use a ¼" seam allowance to stitch only along both sides of the bag and across the bottom edge. (Fig. 12)

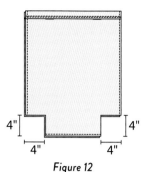

Figure 12

2 Repeat Step 1 with the two Lining rectangles, this time leaving a gap of 6" on the bottom edge, backstitching at the beginning and end of each stitch line. (Fig. 13)

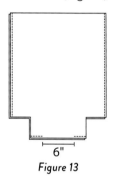

Figure 13

3 Pinch the two layers of the bag apart at the cut corners from Step 1, aligning the side seams and creating a flat edge with two nested seams at the center. Sew along this edge to box the corners of the bag (Fig. 14). Repeat for the opposite corner and both bottom corners of the Exterior.

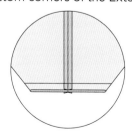

Figure 14

4 Turn the assembled Exterior right side out and press. Slip into the assembled Lining with the right sides facing and the raw edges aligned. Pin or clip in place, aligning the side seams and ensuring the Handles are tucked neatly out of the way inside the bag. Stitch around the upper edge. (Fig. 15)

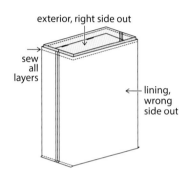

Figure 15

5 Turn the bag right side out through the gap in the Lining from Step 2. Press the top seam towards the Contrast strip, then push the Lining back down inside the Exterior. Press the edge again to create a nice sharp crease, then topstitch around the top of the bag. (Fig. 16)

Figure 16

6 Pull the Handles up so that the Handle Lining is facing the right side of the Contrast strip (Fig. 17). Pin or clip in place. Where the Handle overlaps the Contrast strip, stitch a rectangle with an 'X' inside it through all the layers. Repeat for the opposite side and the second Handle.

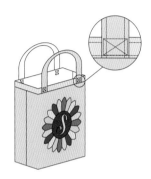

Figure 17

7 Pull the Lining back outside the bag and machine or hand stitch the gap in the Lining closed.

Sling your Shopper over your bike handle and ride into town!

WINDSWEPT

The appliqué in this quilt is worked using the hand-needleturn method (see pages 112–114 for my method as well as tips), which is how I prefer to do all my appliqué. I think that the easiest way to make the templates for this quilt is to laminate them. It can be difficult to trace the lettering accurately, and they are also quite difficult to cut from template plastic, as there are so many little curves and edges.

I'll also mention that this is advanced appliqué. If you haven't tried needleturn appliqué before, you will find the sharp turns and inside points a bit difficult. Take care to use a tightly woven, good-quality patchwork fabric to help you, and make SURE you finger press all the edges of your appliqué!

Finished Size: 42" x 60" (105cm x 150cm)

MATERIALS

2 yards (1.8m) Background fabric

Fat 8th each of 9 Letter fabrics *Note: Some words will not need the whole fat 8th

For the Waves Blocks:
Fabric 1: 12" (30cm) x WOF
Fabric 2: 10" (25cm) x WOF
Fabric 3: 16" (40cm) x WOF
Fabric 4: 10" (25cm) x WOF
Fabric 5: 6" (15cm) x WOF
Fabric 6: 6" (15cm) x WOF

For the Diamond Blocks:
Fabric 7: 10" (25cm) x WOF
Fabric 8: 6" (15cm) x WOF

For the Economy Blocks:
Fabric 9: 4" (10cm) x WOF
Fabric 10: 4" (10cm) x WOF

16" (40cm) x WOF for Binding fabric

4 yards (3.7m) of Backing Fabric

50" x 68" (1.25m x 1.7m) rectangle of Batting

Several large pieces of template plastic, or a laminating machine (see page 66)

Scissors for fabric and plastic

Liquid appliqué glue

Milliners needles #10

Small, sharp embroidery scissors

Silver gel pen

50 or 80 weight cotton threads to match your appliqué fabrics

White chalk pencil

NOTE Since each Ocean block differs in fabric placement, I recommend cutting the fabrics for one block at a time. Alternately, consider placing the pieces for each block on a separate paper plate and label each with the corresponding block number to keep organized.

CUTTING

From the Background Fabric, cut:

(1) 42½" x 26½" rectangle for the appliqué panel

(1) 14½" x WOF strip. Subcut into:
    (1) 14½" x 30½" rectangle
    (1) 14½" x 4½" rectangle

(1) 8½" x WOF strip. Subcut into:
    (1) 8½" x 6½" rectangle
    (2) 8½" x 4½" rectangles
    (1) 8½" x 2½" rectangle

(9) 1½" A squares

(3) 3¼" squares. Subcut twice along the diagonals into:
    9 B triangles (discard 3)

(5) 2⅞" squares. Subcut once along the diagonal into:
    9 C triangles (discard 1)

(3) 5¼" squares. Subcut twice along the diagonals into:
    9 D triangles (discard 3)

(5) 4⅞" squares. Subcut once along the diagonal into:
    9 E triangles (discard 1)

From Fabric 1, cut:

(6) 1½" A squares

(2) 3¼" squares. Subcut twice along the diagonals into:
    6 B triangles (discard 2)

(4) 2⅞" squares. Subcut once along the diagonal into:
    6 C triangles and 1 half D triangle (discard 1)

(2) 5¼" squares. Subcut twice along the diagonals into:
    5 D triangles (discard 3)

(3) 4⅞" squares. Subcut once along the diagonal into:
    5 E triangles (discard 1)

3 Pattern G and 1 G reversed triangles (see pattern on page 125)

From Fabric 2, cut:

(5) 1½" A squares

(1) 2⅜" square. Subcut once along the diagonal into:
  1 half B triangle (discard 1)

(2) 3¼" squares. Subcut twice along the diagonals into:
  5 B triangles (discard 3)

(3) 2⅞" squares. Subcut once along the diagonal into:
  6 C triangles

(2) 5¼" squares. Subcut twice along the diagonals into:
  6 D triangles (discard 2)

(3) 4⅞" squares. Subcut once along the diagonal into:
  6 E triangles
  2 Pattern G triangles
  1 G reversed triangle

From Fabric 3, cut:

(6) 1½" A squares

(1) 2⅜" square. Subcut once along the diagonal into:
  1 half B triangle (discard 1)

(2) 3¼" squares. Subcut twice along the diagonals into:
  5 B triangles (discard 3)

(6) 2⅞" squares. Subcut once along the diagonal into:
  5 C and 1 half D triangles

(2) 5¼" squares. Subcut twice along the diagonals into:
  5 D triangles (discard 3)

(3) 4⅞" squares. Subcut once along the diagonal into:
  6 E triangles
  4 Pattern G triangles
  3 G reversed triangles

From Fabric 4, cut:

(4) 1½" A squares

(1) 3¼" square. Subcut twice along the diagonals into:
  4 B triangles

(2) 2⅞" squares. Subcut once along the diagonal into:
  4 C triangles

(1) 5¼" square. Subcut twice along the diagonals into:
  4 D triangles

(2) 4⅞" squares. Subcut once along the diagonal into:
  4 E triangles
  1 Pattern G triangle
  1 G reversed triangle

From Fabric 5, cut:

(2) 1½" A squares

(1) 3¼" square. Subcut twice along the diagonals into:
  2 B triangles (discard 2)

(1) 2⅞" square. Subcut once along the diagonal into:
  2 C triangles

(1) 5¼" square. Subcut twice along the diagonals into:
  2 D triangles (discard 2)

(1) 4⅞" square. Subcut once along the diagonal into:
  2 E triangles

From Fabric 6, cut:

(2) 1½" A squares

(1) 3¼" square. Subcut twice along the diagonals into:
  2 B triangles (discard 2)

(1) 2⅞" square. Subcut once along the diagonal into:
  2 C triangles

(1) 5¼" square. Subcut twice along the diagonals into:
  2 D triangles (discard 2)

(1) 4⅞" square. Subcut once along the diagonal into:
  2 E triangles

From Fabric 7, cut:

7 Pattern F diamonds (see pattern on page 120)

1 Pattern H half diamond (see pattern on page 125)

From Fabric 8, cut:

7 Pattern G triangles

8 reversed G triangles

From Fabric 9, cut:

(2) 3¼" squares

(1) 2½" x 4½" rectangle

From Fabric 10, cut:

(4) 3" squares. Subcut once along the diagonal into:
  8 triangles
(2) 2½" squares

From the Binding fabric, cut:

(6) 2½" x WOF strips

From the Backing fabric, cut:

(2) 68" x WOF rectangles. Remove selvedges and join along the length. Press the seam open.

PREPARATION

I recommend using an overlock or zigzag stitch around the edge of the 42½" x 26½" Background rectangle. Take care not to change the measurement of the piece when you do. This stitching helps to keep the raw edges from fraying due to the frequent handling required to execute this very complicated appliqué.

MAKING THE APPLIQUÉ

1 Transfer each word or letter onto paper to create a pattern, then create templates using your favorite method (see page 66 for my suggestions).

2 Using a silver gel pen, trace around each word or letter template onto the right side of your selected Letter fabric with the templates facing up.

3 Cut around the drawn lines from Step 2 a scant ¼" from the gel pen lines, but don't cut the negative space away from inside the letters. See page 67 for tips on how to prep the appliqué. (Fig. 1)

> **TIP** *Waiting to cut away the fabric from within each letter makes it much easier to handle each word. With all the spaces cut out, the appliqué would become a big piece of stretchy fabric spaghetti, making it very difficult to place the appliqué pieces without them stretching out of shape.*

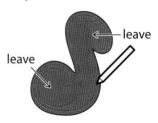

leave

leave

Figure 1

ALIGNING THE APPLIQUÉ

1 Using the white chalk pencil and acrylic ruler, measure 8", 15" and 22" away from the top raw edge of the 42½" x 26½" Background rectangle. Draw three horizontal lines across the width of the panel to act as a guide for positioning the appliqué.

2 Refer to the Assembly Diagram (see page 78) for overall word placement. On a flat surface, position the first row of appliqué right side up along the 8" chalk line. It is important to use the silver gel pen line NOT the cut seam allowance for alignment, as this is where your word will actually be stitched. The first letter 'S' should be 3½" away from the left edge, and the last appliqué on this line finishes 3½" from the right edge. Start by placing the first and last appliqué pieces in each row. This helps in establishing an accurate fit for everything in between.

> **TIP** *Placing a pin through the gel pen line of your appliqué helps line everything up. Don't glue anything down at this stage. Be sure to place all the cut appliqué pieces so that you can see them as a whole and adjust them slightly if desired.*

3 Repeat Step 2 for the second line of appliqué using the 15" chalk line from Step 1 and beginning 9½" away from the left edge of the Background rectangle.

4 Repeat Step 2 for the third line of appliqué using the 22" chalk line from Step 1 and beginning 7½" away from the left edge of the Background rectangle.

5 With all of the appliqué positioned, lift only the edges of the shapes (don't pick them back up!) and place small dots of liquid appliqué glue on the wrong side of the thickest parts of the letters, staying at least ¼" away from the silver gel pen lines. Any sections of the letters that are too thin for gluing, thread baste using longish tacking stitches.

> **TIP** *Remember that the glue will squish out when you press it down, and you need to be able to turn the edges under. If in doubt, use basting stitches instead.*

PIECING THE BLOCKS

I strongly recommend arranging and making one Ocean Block at a time using the Block Diagrams as a guide for fabric placement. I also suggest pinning the block number to the finished blocks (or place the pieces on a design wall in order) so that you don't lose track of which block goes where in the design.

THE OCEAN BLOCKS

1 Create a 4-Patch using (4) 1½" A squares. (Fig. 2)

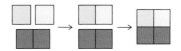

Figure 2

2 Attach a B triangle to one side of the assembled 4-Patch from Step 1.

> **TIP** *Finger press a little crease in the middle of the diagonal edge of the Fabric B triangle, and align it with the center seam of the 4-Patch. This helps maintain alignment.*

3 Press the seam towards the triangle. Repeat Step 2 on the opposite side of the 4-Patch. (Fig. 3)

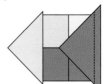

Figure 3

4 Repeat Steps 2–3 for the remaining corners of the 4-Patch and press. (Fig. 4)

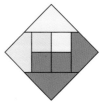

Figure 4

5 Repeat Steps 2–4 using the C triangles and the assembled unit from Step 4 as the center. (Fig. 5)

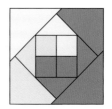

Figure 5

6 Repeat Step 5 using the D triangles and the assembled unit from Step 5 as the center. (Fig. 6)

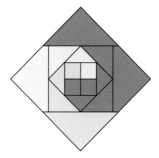

Figure 6

7 Finally, repeat Step 5 using the E triangles. Take care to press towards the triangles. Match the center creases and follow the color scheme as you go.

8 Assemble the remaining seven Ocean Blocks and one half-Ocean Block (using the half B and half D triangles) in the same manner. Refer to the assembly diagrams below for guidance in fabric placement.

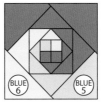

Ocean Block 1

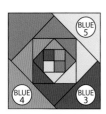

Ocean Block 2

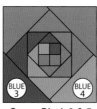

Ocean Block 3 & 5

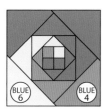

Ocean Block 4

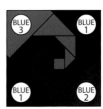

Ocean Block 6

Ocean Block 7

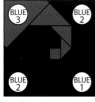

Ocean Block 8

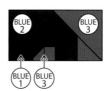

Half-Ocean Block 9

THE ECONOMY BLOCKS

1 Sew a 3" triangle to one side of a 3¼" square.

2 Press the seam towards the triangle, and then repeat Step 1 on the opposite side of the square. (Fig. 7)

Figure 7

3 Repeat Step 2 for the remaining two corners of the square and press.

Blocks 10 & 11

4 To make a half-block for Block 12, place a 2½" square at one end of the 2½" x 4½" rectangle, as shown. Sew along the diagonal and trim to leave a ¼" seam allowance. Press towards the triangle. Repeat at the opposite end of the rectangle.

THE DIAMOND BLOCKS

1 Attach 2 G triangles to the opposite sides of an F diamond. (Fig. 8)

Figure 8

2 Press the seams towards the triangles, and then repeat Step 1 on the remaining 2 opposite sides of the diamond, using the reversed G triangles. (Fig. 9)

Figure 9

3 Repeat to create a total of seven Diamond Blocks referencing the assembly diagrams for fabric placement. Use the K triangle to make Block 20.

Block 13 & 14   *Block 15*

Block 16   *Block 17*

Block 18   *Block 19*

Block 20

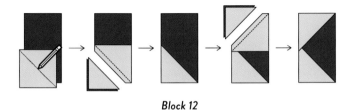

Block 12

ASSEMBLING THE QUILT TOP

1 Referencing the Assembly Diagram, arrange and sew the appliqué panel, Ocean Blocks and Background rectangles into three sections. The top section is the appliqué panel, the middle is Ocean Block 1 with three Background pieces and the bottom section is composed of the remaining blocks and Background pieces.

2 Sew the sections together as shown.

FINISHING

Layer the Backing rectangle with the wrong side up, then the Batting, and finally the quilt top right side up. Baste, quilt, and attach the binding using your favorite method.

QUILTING

I hand quilted WINDSWEPT using 12 weight thread in swirling patterns on and above the waves. I added a lighthouse on the right with its beams of light cutting across the quilt. I outline-quilted the words, and finally quilted vertical lines in the top section to represent rain.

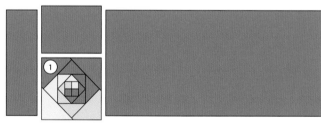

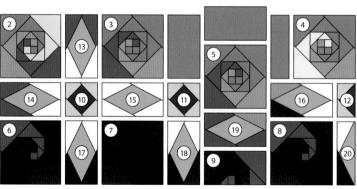

Assembly Diagram

5

THE

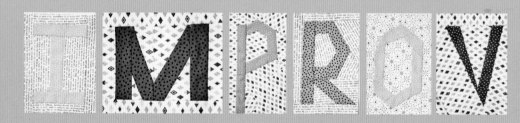

ALPHABET

LET'S PRACTICE!
THE IMPROV ALPHABET

No grids or templates here! Don't be intimidated—all you need to know is how to sew a straight line and how to write. There are a few rules though. Lots of improv is just about whacking it all together any old how. To make these shapes look like readable letters, there are a few guidelines to follow though, so I suppose this isn't TRUE improv—I like to call it "improv with intent."

All the improv letters are stitched almost the same way as you would write them. Your blank page is the negative space—or the background fabric. For example, to write an 'a', you start with a circle around the negative space. Then you put the "stem" down the side. Our eye sees the line, but the letter is formed also by the space around it. That's what we're going to do here.

LOWERCASE 'A'

1 Gather some fabric to use for the Background (or negative space) and Letter fabrics. A fat quarter of each should be enough to get started. Cut one or two strips about 1½" wide from the Letter fabric and cut it into 6–8" lengths.

> **TIP** If working from yardage, a single WOF strip will be enough to create nearly any letter unless you have very detailed shaping!

You can use strips cut from scraps or precuts or whatever you have on hand! Be sure to cut straight parallel edges for these beginning strips, just as you would for standard patchwork. This helps to control all the bias that is created by the improv.

2 Cut a few strips about 3" x 22" from the Background fat quarter or a single 3" wide strip if using yardage.

> **TIP** I say "about" a lot in this alphabet. Although I make the widths of all my letter strips the same, the block size doesn't really matter. A word of caution though, if you have never pieced like this before, I do recommend that you cut a strip on the wider side rather than narrower. If you have a tendency to think you're going to "waste" fabric, be a little generous with yourself

in this process. Start by using a fabric you are comfortable practicing with instead of something you love. Trying to be frugal with the Background on improv letters will only lead to patching little pieces back in if the block can't be squared up.

3 Cut a square from the Background fabric for the negative space of the 'a'. This cut doesn't have to be accurate, or even square. Just a shape. You can even just lop it off the strip with scissors. (Fig. 1)

Figure 1

4 Before we begin piecing the 'a', let's remember what it is like to write an 'a'. When you start, you begin at the top of the curve at the front of the letter (Fig. 2). We are going to follow the same line of writing but by piecing our Letter fabric strips instead.

Figure 2

5 Sew a 1½" strip of Letter fabric at an angle across the top right corner of the Background center (Fig. 3). Do not be tempted to cut the angle into the rectangle first before stitching. This creates extra bias edges to work with, that risk distorting the block. Trim any Background fabric to ¼" away from the seam and press towards the Letter fabric.

Figure 3

TIP *Trimming down seams is incredibly important in this alphabet. If you don't trim that extra piece beyond the ¼" seam*

allowance, you have a letter than can be five or six layers of fabric thick! This means your block will look lumpy and awkward and will be nasty to quilt through. Stitch, TRIM, then press.

6 Sew another Letter strip at a different angle to the top left side of the rectangle, forming the top curve of the 'a' (Fig. 4). Remember, you are mimicking how you would write this letter, so follow the curve of the 'a' using the Letter fabric strips. Trim all the fabric ¼" away from the stitch line and press.

Figure 4

7 Sew a Letter strip along the left side of the front of the 'a' (Fig. 5), trim and press.

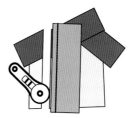

Figure 5

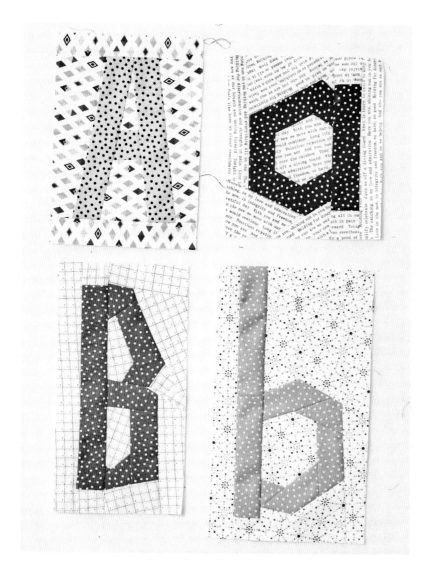

8 Add two more Letter strips in the same manner to complete the curve of your 'a'. (Fig. 6)

Figure 6

9 Before adding the final Letter strip to form the straight side or stem of the 'a', subcut some rectangles from your 3" Background fabric strips. Attach these to the assembled unit from Step 8 in the same manner. Begin in the same place at the top of the letter and follow the curve around. When completed, the assembled unit should look like a 'c' surrounded by Background fabric (Fig. 7). Make sure to trim away the excess fabric to keep your seams at ¼" as you work.

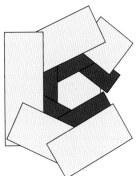

Figure 7

10 Using an acrylic ruler, trim a clean straight line along the right side of the assembled unit from Step 9, where you want the stem to go. Make sure that you cut through the Background and the Letter fabric so that you have a straight line to attach the next piece to. (Fig. 8)

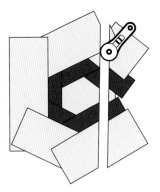

Figure 8

TIP *If you were making a letter 'c', you would sew more Background fabric along this open edge to surround the letter and it would be finished.*

11 Cut a length of a Letter strip long enough to be the stem of the 'a'. There will be a ¼" seam allowance off each short end when the Background fabric is added. Account for this when trimming the final Letter strip.

12 Cut two small pieces of Background fabric the same width as your Letter strip from Step 11. Add these to the top and bottom of the Letter strip and attach the assembled unit to the straight trimmed edge from Step 10. (Fig. 9)

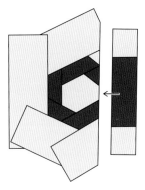

Figure 9

13 Square the letter up and you are all done!

LOWERCASE 'E'

Ready for a more challenging letter? Not all letters are the same. Some are more difficult and require two segments to be joined together, such as the lowercase 'e' and 's'. Let's practice with the lowercase letter 'e'.

As you may have noticed in sewing the letter 'a', each letter has an element that determines the height or width of the letter. For an 'i' or an 'l' that is obviously the length of their straight line. For curved letters, or letters like a 'v' or a 'w', or the 'a' we just practiced, the cut size of the piece of Background fabric that forms the center determines the finished letter size.

Cut the fabric for the negative space around 2" or even smaller for little letters and cut the pieces closer to 4" or even bigger for the larger ones.

A little experimentation with a few letters will give you the idea of where to begin to suit the project you are piecing.

1 Gather some fabric to use for the Background (or negative space) and Letter fabrics. Cut one or two strips about 1½" wide from the Letter fabric and cut it into 6–8" lengths.

2 To begin, cut two small rectangles from the Background fabric. Remember that the rectangle will be the size of the top curve of the 'e' and the slightly smaller bottom portion (Fig. 10). The combined height of these two pieces will be roughly the height of your letter. Set the bottom aside for now.

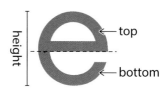

Figure 10

3 For the top section we will work with the larger Background rectangle from Step 2. We will follow the curve of the upper part of the 'e' as we did for the practice 'a' (Fig. 11), except this time, the entire Background is surrounded by Letter fabric.

Figure 11

4 Sew Letter strips around the top edges of the Background rectangle to create the top curve of the 'e' with a final Letter strip at the bottom. Be sure to keep those seam allowances to ¼". Add the Background rectangles to the outer edges of the assembled unit. (Fig. 12)

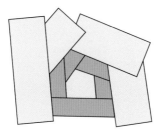

Figure 12

5 Repeat Step 4 to create the bottom half of the 'e' using the smaller Background rectangle from Step 2. With the right sides up, position the bottom half of the 'e' slightly over the top half until you are happy with the angle along which the two sections will be pieced together. Using an acrylic ruler, cut straight along the angle you like, through all of the layers. Don't be afraid! I promise it works, and it's only fabric! :)

6 When you have a straight line, align the two sections right sides facing, pin and sew them together. (Fig. 13)

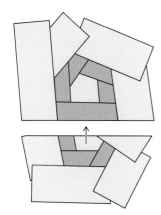

Figure 13

Many of the letters for the Improv Alphabet are made in sections, by completing one part of the letter and then adding to it or altering it. An uppercase 'S' for example, is the top half surrounded by background, the bottom half surrounded by background, trimming them at an angle, and joining them together. (Fig. 14)

Figure 14

ESTABLISHING SPACING BETWEEN LETTERS

Once all the letters to spell each word have been pieced, line them up ready to sew together to make a word. One of the most important things about working with letters is establishing the spacing between them. Consider for example this sentence:

Today I went to quilting class.

Our eyes are trained to see the combination of letters and spaces that we know so well, and our eyes tell us, quickly and easily, what the letters say.

If you change the spacing of the letters, things aren't so clear:

To dayl wen tto qui ltingclass.

To prevent this spacing crisis, each word in an Improv Alphabet sentence is going to be its own block. Keeping the spacing between each letter consistent, and the spacing between each word the same, ensures that it won't matter if some letters are a bit 'misshapen'. Our eyes will read the correct words as long as the spacing between them is consistent.

When all of the letters for a word are pieced, some of the letters may be different sizes and shapes. (Fig. 15)

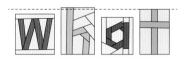

Figure 15

In order to bring them all to a similar size, simply stitch additional Background fabric around the smaller finished letter blocks or trim Background fabric away from the larger ones to make each letter a block of the same size (Fig. 16). This way, each letter next in line can be sewn in a row in the word.

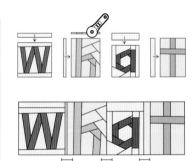

equal space between letters

Figure 16

Again, don't worry about making each word the same height or dimension. When joining all these word blocks into a quilt, they are assembled exactly the same way. You can see an example of that in A FAIR QUESTION on page 96.

My Improv Alphabet is so freeing and joyful! Once you get the hang of it you can just create as you go along, without having to think or measure. Don't be intimidated by rigid patchwork rules, or "wasted" fabric. Jump in, go as wonky as you like and give it a go. It's a whole new way of working that will enrich your stitching.

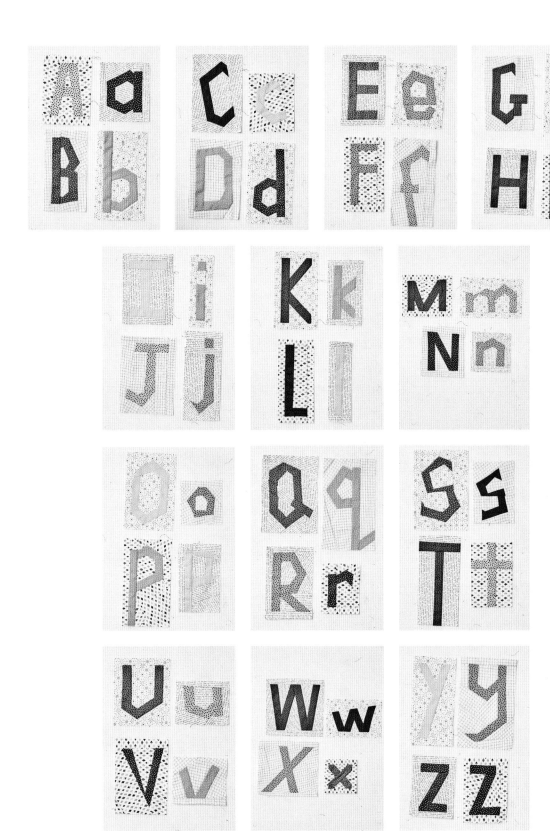

BITS AND PIECES POUCHES

I don't know about you, but I have a lot of bits and pieces. I'm always on the lookout for somewhere else to stash my stuff! These Bits and Pieces Pouches are the perfect place to store the essential things you need to cart around with you.

I can already see I'm going to have to make more. You can customize the words to go with what's inside, or add someone's name for a personal touch.

Finished Size: 14" wide x 7½" high (35cm x 19cm)

MATERIALS
*Materials listed are for two pouches

10" (25cm) x WOF Letter Fabric

Fat quarter of Exterior Fabric for the BITS pouch

Fat quarter of Exterior Fabric for the PIECES pouch

20" (50cm) x WOF of Lining Fabric

Various Scraps of three different fabrics for BITS pouch Background totaling approximately 12" (30cm) x WOF

Various Scraps of four different fabrics for PIECES pouch Background totaling approximately 12" (30cm) x WOF

16" x 36" (40cm x 90cm) rectangle of fusible fleece

(2) 11" zippers

Sharp pencil

CUTTING
Photocopy the Pouch pattern (see page 126) and cut out to create a template.

From the Letter Fabric, cut:
   (10) 1" x WOF strips. Subcut into 6"strips

From each Exterior Fabric, cut:
   (1) 15" x 1½" rectangle

   (1) 16" x 9" rectangle for the pouch back

From the Lining Fabric, cut:
   (4) 16" x 9" rectangles

From the Background Scraps, cut a variety of rectangles each at least 2½" x 3"

From the Fusible Fleece, cut:
   (4) 16" x 9" rectangles

Use a ¼" seam allowance unless otherwise noted.

ASSEMBLING THE FRONT PANELS
1 Following the instructions beginning on page 82 for piecing the Improv Alphabet, piece the lowercase letters 'b-i-t-s' and 'p-i-e-c-e-s'. These letters need to be small, so that they fit within the Pouch template.

Make sure that the units of each letter that establish the size of the finished block (usually the negative space) are small. For example, the Background Scrap I started with at the center of my 'e' is only about 2½" square.

The thin Letter strips will also help yield smaller letters.

TIP I used the different colors randomly when I pieced each letter to reinforce the scrappy patchwork effect.

2 When adding Background Scraps around each finished letter, be generous with the space above and below so that it's tall enough to create the Front Panel of the pouches.

NOTE I made the PIECES pouch using the solid blue Background Scraps and the BITS using pinks, corals and oranges.

3 Trim and join the letters together to form each word, making certain that the assembled units are going to be large enough to cover the Pouch template. If they aren't, add some more Background Scraps to the perimeter. The assembled Front Panel will need to be about 8½" x 15". (Fig. 1)

Figure 1

4 Working on one pouch at a time, make a horizontal cut along the top edge of the Front Panel from Step 3 to create a straight line for assembly. With the right sides together and aligning the long raw edges, stitch the 15" x 1½" Exterior rectangle to the top of the Front Panel (Fig. 2), forming the Accent Strip. Press the seam towards the Accent Strip.

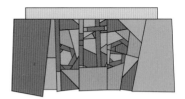

Figure 2

5 With the right side of the assembled Front Panel facing up, align the top edge of the Pouch template with the raw edge of the attached Accent strip. Trace around the template onto the Front Panel using a sharp pencil.

> **TIP** *Double check that there is at least ½" between the traced Pouch line and all of your pieced letters to accommodate the seam allowance.*

PREPARING THE PANELS

1 On the right side of the Lining and Back rectangles, trace around the Pouch template using a sharp pencil. Set the Lining aside.

2 Following the manufacturer's instructions, adhere a rectangle of fusible fleece to the wrong sides of the Back rectangle and the Front Panel. If necessary, trim the Fleece to fit the Front Panel before fusing.

> **TIP** *I recommend pressing with the fabric side up, in case the fusible adhesive is accidentally positioned the wrong way. This will avoid getting adhesive on your iron, but won't save your pressing surface. Always double check that the adhesive side (the rougher side) of the fusible fleece is facing the wrong side of the fabric.*

3 If desired, add any quilting to the fused Front and/or Back Panels.

4 Cut along the traced template line from Step 1 on the Back Panel. Repeat with the two Lining rectangles.

ATTACHING THE ZIPPER

1 Position the Front Panel right side up, center the zipper (facing down with the zipper pull on the left side) on top, and then place a Lining panel wrong side up. Pin or clip to secure the layers. (Fig. 3)

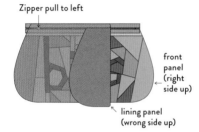

Zipper pull to left

front panel (right side up)

lining panel (wrong side up)

Figure 3

2 Using the zipper foot attachment on your machine, sew along the upper edge of the zipper tape.

3 Position the Front Panel and Lining wrong sides together. Press away from the zipper. Edgestitch along the right side of the Front Panel, close to the fold. (Fig. 4)

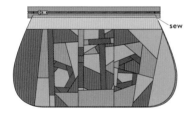

sew

Figure 4

4 Repeat Steps 1–3 for the Back and remaining Lining Panel. Unzip the zipper halfway. (Fig. 5)

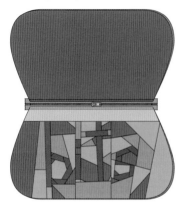

Figure 5

ASSEMBLING THE BAG

1 Switch back to a regular foot. Position both Exterior Panels right sides facing on one side of the half-open zipper and the Lining Panels on the other. Both right sides should be facing together. Pin in place to secure the layers and ensure the zipper teeth are lying on the Linings. Starting in the middle of the long side of the Lining, sew around the perimeter, leaving a 3" opening for turning the bag. (Fig. 6)

Figure 6

2 To keep those curves a nice shape, trim the seam allowance on them back to a scant ¼". Turn the bag right side out and smooth out the curved base of the bag using a chopstick or similar blunt object. Hand or machine sew the gap in the Lining closed. Push the Lining inside the Exterior. Press.

3 Carefully push out the corners near the zipper. On the inside of the bag, hand stitch a few tacking stitches to secure the Lining to the Exterior. This will help retain the bag's shape.

4 Repeat for the second pouch.

Now you can collect all your bits and pieces that finally have a home!

A FAIR QUESTION

"What delight! What felicity! Adieu to disappointment and spleen. What are men to rocks and mountains?"
—*Jane Austen,*
Pride and Prejudice, 1813

One of my favorite things to do is curl up under a quilt on a cold day with a cup of tea and a book. What better quilt for my reading spot, than one with a quote from my favorite book?

All the strips for the letters are 1½" cut. If you want to make very large letters they might look a bit spindly, and you may want to increase your strips to 2½". For smaller letters, I cut my strips to 1" wide.

Finished size: Will vary. Mine is 75" x 77" (191cm x 196cm)

MATERIALS

NOTE *Materials listed are approximate due to the improvisational nature of this quilt. The measurements provided are approximate for a quilt the same size as mine.*

Various Scraps in a single hue measuring approximately (1) 1½" x WOF for each letter. I used from light pink to dark maroon/purple

A large assortment of dark-medium fabrics in a single hue for the Background Letters—(1) 3" strip x WOF strip for a complex letter, approximately

Fat quarters and half yards of very dark through to almost white in a single hue for Background totaling approximately 3½ yards (3.15m)

(22) 4–6" squares for Shooting Star triangles, or approximately 12" (30cm) x WOF

1 fat quarter for the Moon

(5) 5" squares for the Stars

8" (20cm) x WOF strips of each of five or more Trees

(1) 4" (10cm) x WOF strip for the Trunks

24" (60cm) x WOF Binding Fabric approximately (I used leftovers of all the different yellows from my Shooting Stars joined together)

5 yards (4.5m) of Backing fabric

83" x 85" (210cm x 215cm) of Batting

Silver gel pen

Scissors for paper and fabric

Template plastic

Appliqué needles

Cotton thread to match the appliqué fabrics

> **TIP** *With improv piecing, it is always ok to add another bit of fabric in here and there, to make any element in this quilt top the size you need. Just remember to trim a straight edge first to ensure a straight, flat seam.*

PIECING THE LETTERS

While you can begin by piecing any element on this quilt top first, I recommend beginning with the letters.

1 To create the first word, 'W-h-a-t', follow the Improv Alphabet piecing instructions (see pages 82–87). From a selection of Letter scraps, cut a variety of lengths 1½" wide. Cut a strip about 3" wide from some of the Background fabrics.

Piece all of the letters separately and don't worry too much about what size they are in relation to each other. We practiced creating consistent spacing between letters in our Improv Alphabet. But here I wanted a less linear look, so I pieced in various pieces of Background fabric around each letter. The only real rules to follow with this alphabet are:

1 Make sure each letter has 90-degree edges when it has been trimmed

2 Piece the letters together into a word that forms a block with 90-degree edges

3 Piece each section of the quilt according to straight lines

2 When a complete word is pieced, begin to add or trim away Background fabric so that all the letters end up the same size. In Figure 1, add

Background fabric to the top of the 'W' and the top and bottom of the 'a' in order to make them all the same size as the 't'. Trim the 'h' down to fit. At this time, check your spacing between each letter too. In Figure 1, I added 1" or so to the side of the 'W' so that the 'h' doesn't butt right up against it at the top of the blocks. Whenever possible, cut the pieces of Background fabric you are adding on the straight-of- grain, to provide a straight edge. This ensures that the blocks won't lose their shape from the bias in the improv.

Figure 1

TIP *If you want the letters to sit on a straight line, trim so that all the bottoms of the letter blocks are aligned. If you want the letters to look uneven, add some Background fabrics to the bottom of each.*

3 Repeat Steps 1–2 to piece each of the word blocks.

TIP *My version transitions in background color from a very dark (almost black) navy at the top, to almost white blue at the bottom of the quilt. I was trying to capture the look of a mountain sky fading into the night. If you'd like to* do the same, the top words *should be in your darkest background fabrics with the lightest pink letter fabrics. The letter fabrics should get progressively lighter in background and darker in letters, so that the bottom of the quilt has the lightest background fabric with the darkest letter fabric.*

ASSEMBLING THE SHOOTING STAR TRAIL PANELS

The trails of Shooting Stars are improv flying geese. I have nine geese in one trail and 13 in the other—you may need more or fewer depending on how large your geese turn out to be and how long you want your trails.

1 Begin with a randomly cut Star fabric somewhere between 2½" square to about 6" x 3". This allows for long and skinny or short and squat trails. The triangles are all pieced using 3" strips of the darkest Background fabrics.

2 Position the Background and the Star fabric rectangles right sides together, with the Background rectangle on top at an angle somewhere between 30-and 60-degrees. There should be at least ½" of Background fabric extending over both edges of the Star piece. Stitch (Fig. 2). Trim the excess Star fabric ¼" away from the seam and press the seam to one side.

Figure 2

3 With the right sides together, position another strip of Background fabric diagonally over the assembled unit from Step 2. Again, check that there is at least ½" of Background fabric extending over both ends. Stitch and trim the excess and press the seam to one side. (Fig. 3)

Figure 3

4 With the overlapping Background strips at the left and the raw edge of the Star fabric at the right, make two parallel cuts along the sides. The left edge should be trimmed ¼" outside the point where the two Background strips intersect and there should be at least ¼" of fabric extending beyond the bottom two points of the triangle.

5 Trim the top and bottom of the unit from Step 4 to make a strip (Fig. 4). Trim the strip ends to make a rectangle.

Figure 4

6 Make as many of the flying geese as desired in the same manner. Don't worry about what size or shape they are relative to each other, just make sure that they are all some form of a triangle, trimmed to a rectangle. (Fig. 5)

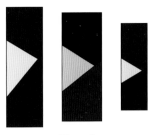

Figure 5

7 Arrange the assembled flying geese on the floor or the design wall above 'What are men'. Take a moment to evaluate whether there needs to be more or fewer triangles at this stage.

8 Sew strips of Background fabric to the top and bottom of each rectangle (Fig. 6). Each strip should be the same width as the flying geese rectangle, but the length doesn't have to be the same at this step.

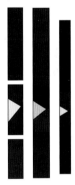

Figure 6

9 Begin sewing together the assembled flying geese strips from Step 8 along their long side. Pay attention to the alignment of the Star fabric triangles in an arc or line as desired. (Fig. 7)

Figure 7

10 Two Shooting Star tails may be very close to one another. If the strips are the same width, piece a couple of flying geese within a single strip or shorten the length of the Background strips and form a few sections. This takes a bit of planning. Be prepared to play around with your Star trail units to create smaller blocks that can be easily sewn together as rows or columns as you would in a traditionally pieced quilt top. Reference the Shooting Star Assembly Diagram below to see examples of how I created some of these sections.

ASSEMBLING THE TREE BLOCKS

1 The Tree blocks begin with the Trunk. My Trunks are all cut around about 1½"–2" wide and about 5" or 6" high.

2 Cut two pieces of Background fabric around 4" wide (err on the wider side) and stitch them to either side of the Trunk. (Fig. 8)

Figure 8

TIP *If you are piecing your top using the fading gradient as I did, be mindful of the shade of the Background fabric you are using.*

3 Cut some Tree fabrics into strips around 8" wide and some matching background strips about 6" wide. Position a rectangle of Tree fabric and the Trunk right sides together and at a sharp diagonal beginning at about the middle of the top of the Trunk and angling down to

the side. As with the Shooting Star tails, make sure there is at least ½" of Background fabric extending over both sides. Stitch and trim the excess Background fabric ¼" away from the sewn line. (Fig. 9)

Figure 9

4 Press the seam open and repeat with the other side of the assembled unit from Step 3 and press again.

5 At a sharp angle, trim the sides of the assembled unit from Step 4 to form the tree canopy shape as an inverted 'V'. (Fig. 10)

Figure 10

6 Repeating Steps 3–4, sew two more Background rectangles to the trimmed unit from Step 5. The Background rectangles should meet at the top of the Tree strips in a point, forming a second inverted 'V' shape of Background fabric. (Fig. 11)

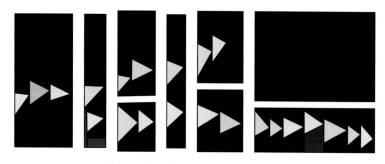

Shooting Star Sample Assembly Diagram

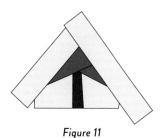

Figure 11

7 Position the assembled unit from Step 6 with the Trunk nearest you. Trim the top of the Background fabric 'V', ¼" away from the intersection of the two Tree strips (Fig. 12). This will help you to position the next canopy of Tree fabric strips without losing the point, if you don't want to that is! It's your choice.

Figure 12

8 Repeat Steps 3–7 until the Tree is as tall as you would like it to be. (Fig. 13)

Figure 13

9 My Trees are all two and three canopies high but you could make them even larger. When all of the piecing for the Trees has been done to get the desired height, position an assembled unit right side up with the Trunk nearest you. Angle an acrylic ruler along the side of the Tree, ¼" outside the end points of as many canopies as possible. Trim, and then repeat with the other side of the Tree. (Fig. 14)

Figure 14

10 Large Background triangles are most easily made by cutting the corners off a fat quarter. Attach these around the trimmed unit from Step 9. Square-up to make a rectangular block with the Tree in the middle.

11 Repeat to make a total of five Tree blocks. (Fig. 15)

Figure 15

ASSEMBLING ROWS 1–3

1 Arrange all the completed blocks on a design wall or on the floor until you are happy with the placement. Row 1 will be assembled first.

> **TIP** *If you are using the same phrase as me, it should read: 'What are men to rocks and mountains?'*

2 The upper portion of the quilt is assembled in straight rows and columns, just like in a traditional quilt. Look to create straight lines for your piecing when adding in Background fabrics to make each block in all the rows the same height. If you are piecing a partial seam, something has gone wrong! Add in Background fabrics as needed to fill in all the gaps.

3 The top row in my quilt top is the Star trail, the second row has 'What are', and the third row has 'men'. My free-hand cut crescent Moon appliqué is 10½" at the widest point, and is positioned above the 'W' in the word 'What'. So that space needs to be at least 11" wide for a good fit.

> **TIP** *The Background pieces are random cuts of a variety of different blues. None of the pieces is measured, as everyone's top will be slightly different, but they ARE all cut on the straight-of-grain, and with straight edges.*

ATTACHING THE APPLIQUÉ

1 From the template plastic or laminate, use the Star pattern (see page 125) and a silver gel pen to trace around the pattern onto the right side of the Star fabric. Repeat for all of the stars (I used five in my version). Cut around the shapes ¼" away from the outer edge of the gel pen line.

> **TIP** It is much easier to attach the appliqué before joining the rest of the rows when using the hand appliqué method.

2 Decide where to place the Stars. I have one at the beginning of a star trail in row 1 and four others scattered around the top where I thought they were needed to fill some space.

3 Using liquid appliqué glue, secure the Stars in place, then needleturn appliqué (see pages 112–114) or appliqué using your favorite method.

4 Referencing the Assembly Diagram on the facing page, join together rows 1 and 2.

5 On a piece of paper, draw a crescent Moon shape to create a pattern. This will have to fit well in the space to the left of the word 'What'.

6 Repeat Steps 1–3 to create a Moon template and appliqué shape. Position the Moon above the 'W' and above the seam between the two assembled rows from Step 4. Appliqué in place.

ASSEMBLING THE SECOND HALF OF THE QUILT TOP

1 Add in Background fabrics to fill any gaps in row 3. The piecing structure should become clear based on the unfinished block sizes. If you are using the same phrase as I did, assemble 'to rocks' into one block, 'mountains' into another and three Tree blocks creating three rows of equal width. Stitch together the rows and press.

2 Repeat with the remaining two Tree blocks and the 'and' to create two rows of equal width. Adding a strip of Background fabric between, stitch together the rows, press and trim to the same height as the unit from Step 1.

3 Use the assembled rows 1 and 2 to establish the width for the two assembled sections from Step 1 and 2.

4 Stitch row 3 to the assembled Row 1-2 unit. Press and square-up if needed.

> **TIP** No matter how carefully you plan, improv quilts often need another square-up once the top is entirely pieced together.

FINISHING

Depending on how large your quilt is, your Backing and Binding fabric quantities may differ from mine. The requirements provided for a quilt the size of mine, include 4" extra all the way around the perimeter of the top to allow for quilting. I used nine strips of Binding, cut 2½" wide, for my quilt.

Layer the Backing rectangle with the wrong side up, then the Batting, and finally the quilt top right side up. Baste, quilt, and attach the binding using your favorite method.

QUILTING

I had A FAIR QUESTION custom machine-quilted by Kat Jones. Kat free-hand quilted a different filler pattern into each section of the quilt, creating a beautiful modern texture behind the improv piecing.

Assembly Diagram

6

CURSIVE BIAS TAPE APPLIQUÉ

Cursive needleturn appliqué like our Back to Black alphabet looks incredible—but sometimes we just want some instant gratification! Bias tape appliqué is down-and-dirty quick if you use the pre-made fusible variety. This project is just the thing to break into that wonderful fat quarter bundle of rainbow solids you've been hoarding.

The letters in this cushion are just my handwriting. If you want to create your own bias tape word, you can write it out yourself—but if you aren't confident enough to do that, try finding a cursive script online being sure to be compliant with any permissions or licenses required. Look for a script that has thin, elegant lines that you can cover with the tape—quite unlike what you want for a needleturn appliqué font.

I like to use the pre-made fusible bias tape that is available in so many lovely colors for these projects. It's easy to use and quick to apply. There are lots of products available that enable you to make your own bias tape as well, using any fabric desired. I like to use a Hera marker to make mine when I want to use a print fabric—and you can see my method in the techniques section (see page 115) if you fancy making your own.

RAINBOW SCRIPT CUSHION

This project is perfect for using one of those beautiful rainbow bundles of solids we all buy and put away and bring out to stroke every now and then! It would look wonderful with a rainbow progression of prints too—pull out favorites from your stash and play with the grading to see what you find.

The Rainbow cushion is lovely for a kid's bedroom, but I'll admit to having to make two—one for my little rainbow-loving niece, and one for me!

Finished size: 25" x 15" (63cm x 38cm)

MATERIALS

(20) 1¾" x 16" strips of Solid Fabric in a rainbow of colors

(1) 2" square of Dot Fabric

(1) 16" x WOF (40cm) rectangle of Backing Fabric

(1) 26" x 16" (65cm x 40cm) rectangle of lightweight Fusible Interfacing

(1) 26" x 16" (65cm x 40cm) cushion insert

4 yards black pre-made ¼"-wide double-fold fusible bias tape OR fabric to make your own plus 4 yards of ¼"-wide fusible web strips

2½ yards of ¼"-diameter black piping cord (optional)

Small piece of template plastic or cardboard

Sharp pencil

Milliners needles if appliquéing by hand

Cotton thread to match the bias tape

CUTTING

From the template plastic, cut:
one Dot Template (see page 124)

From the Backing Fabric, cut:
(1) 13½" x 15½" rectangle

(1) 18½" x 15½" rectangle

Use a ¼" seam allowance unless otherwise noted.

ASSEMBLING THE CUSHION FRONT

1 Decide on the placement of your rainbow of strips.

> **TIP** Not a fan of rainbow order? Select strips that are just in a gradient of a single hue or two instead!

2 Stitch the 20 strips together along their long edge using a scant ¼" seam allowance and press the seams to one side. Make sure you have pressed the panel well.

ATTACHING THE APPLIQUÉ

1 Fold the Rainbow panel in half lengthwise and lightly press a crease at the horizontal center. (Fig. 1)

2 Enlarge the Rainbow pattern on page 124. Using a light box, a well-lit window or a glass table with a lamp under it, place the pieced Rainbow panel right side up on top of the pattern. Align the horizontal center crease and the seams with the pattern's alignment lines. Trace the word onto the panel with a sharp pencil.

3 Remove the protective strip from the back of the bias tape and use a very hot, dry iron to fuse it in place over the drawn line from Step 2. Use the

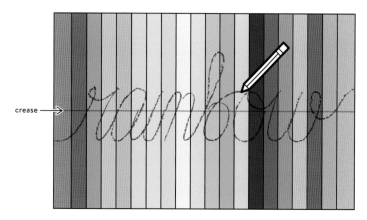

crease →

Figure 1

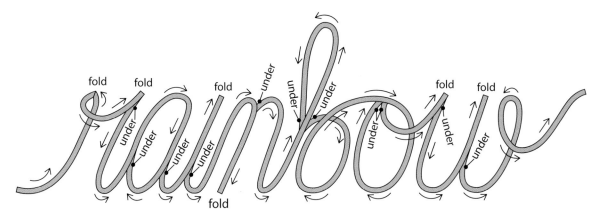

Appliqué Diagram

Appliqué Diagram when you do this to indicate where the pieces should end, fold, or go underneath each other.

4 When approaching a fold, take the tape to the top of the shape, and miter a fold in the tape to make it change direction. (Fig. 2)

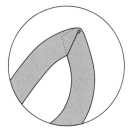

Figure 2

5 When approaching a point where the tape goes underneath, cut the tape at an appropriate angle and position the end underneath the previous piece of tape. Press to secure. (Figs. 3–4)

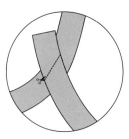

Figure 3

Figure 4

6 When you come to an end of a piece of tape, cut the tape ¼" longer than the line and fuse the end underneath the tape to make a fold. (Figs. 5–6)

Figure 5

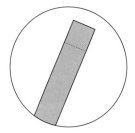

Figure 6

7 Stitch both edges of the tape down. I hand stitched my tape using black thread, but you could easily machine stitch using a blanket stitch.

8 Using the Dot Template, cut a circle from the 2" square of Dot fabric. Using my needleturn appliqué instructions (see pages 112–114), attach the circle above the 'i'.

FINISHING

1 Give the panel a good press with a steam iron, and then follow the manufacturer's instructions to fuse the stabilizer to the wrong side of the assembled Front Panel. Trim to 25½" x 15½".

2 If using the optional piping, make (or buy) 2½ yards of ¼"-diameter piping in black

fabric or another color which matches the bias tape.

3 See the envelope cushion instructions on page 27 for attaching the piping to the Front Panel and adding the two Backing rectangles.

Bring a little sunshine into your favorite corner even on a rainy day!

TOOLS AND THREADS

ESSENTIALS

- Sewing machine in good working order (unless you are a dedicated hand sewer!) and replacement needles. I use a sharp needle, size 70/10, for all my patchwork.

- ¼" (6mm) machine foot to fit your machine. Do consider investing in one of these—they are a little pricey but will make a huge difference to your stitching and will make accurate seams so much easier.

- Dressmaking scissors to be used for cutting fabric only.

- Scissors for cutting paper or plastic.

- Thread snips or small, sharp scissors.

- Seam ripper.

- Straight pins.

- Tape measure.

- Acrylic/Perspex quilter's ruler(s)—it is handy to have two rulers of the same size to assist in cutting strips without having to turn the cutting mat around.

- Rotary cutter (the best you can afford) and replacement blades.

- Self-healing cutting mat.

- Masking tape, for securing the backing fabric to a flat surface and for making straight hand quilting lines without marking your quilt.

- Chalk pencil, sharp pencil and silver gel pen, for marking curved quilting and appliqué lines.

- Quilter's safety pins (if you are pinning quilt layers rather than thread basting).

- Quilter's hoop, for hand quilting (this is not an embroidery hoop).

- Quilter's thimble.

- Needles for appliqué. I use a Milliners needle #10 for my appliqué. I like a long, slim, fine needle with a small eye to assist with tiny stitches and easy turning.

- Needles for hand quilting. I use a crewel embroidery needle #9 for quilting with Perle cotton or Aurifil 12 weight cotton. You need a long, sturdy needle that isn't too thick, with a small eye.

- Liquid appliqué glue, such as Roxanne Glue-Baste-It or Sue Daley Appliqué Glue. This is a washable, acid free glue made especially for appliqué. I never use glue sticks for needleturn appliqué because pulling the stick along the bias of the fabric can stretch small pieces.

FAVORITES

- Hera marker—for making bias tape using my method (see page 129) and for marking quilting lines or cursive words for going over with bias tape without using a pen or pencil.

- Fine patchwork pins—more expensive than regular pins, but so slim and fine that they allow pinning without puckering the fabric.

- Needle rest—contains a magnet that allows you to lay down your needle without putting it through your work.

- Wonder Clips—I use these little marvels for everything from holding down a binding, to English paper piecing. They are also very useful for keeping cut pieces and stacks of blocks together.

- Turning tool—something with a long, pointy end can be invaluable for helping you feed points under your machine foot cleanly. There are many tools on the market for this; I have a beautiful porcupine quill given to me by a quilting friend.

- A door peephole/peeper, easily and inexpensively bought from a hardware store, can be useful for viewing your blocks from a distance while standing up close. Doing this will help you balance tone, color and scale.

SPECIALTY RULERS

All the quilts in this book can be made using a standard 24 in. (60cm) quilter's ruler and the templates provided. You could also use a specialty ruler made for cutting diamond shapes, half-square and quarter-square triangles. Although I have not usually listed them in the requirements for each project, these rulers make cutting much quicker and easier—if you wish to use them, by all means do so. They are usually sold with detailed instructions for their use and are widely available from your local patchwork shop, or from my website.

HALF-SQUARE TRIANGLE RULER

A half-square ruler, also called a 45-degree triangle ruler, is useful but not strictly necessary for cutting half-square triangles. You can, of course, cut these triangles using a standard quilter's ruler by cross-cutting strips into squares, then cross-cutting each square in half on one diagonal, resulting in two half-square triangles. The size of the square that you cut when cutting half-square triangles in this way should always be 7/8" (2.2 cm) larger than the desired finished size of the triangle. But depending on your preferred method, you may wish to cut them larger and trim them down to size.

Specialized half-square triangle rulers, however, have already allowed for the seam allowance at the point of the triangle, thus eliminating the "ears" on the seam. This means that if you are using a half-square triangle ruler, you will cut the triangles from a strip of fabric rather than from squares, and the size of your strip should be only ½" (12 mm) larger than the desired finished size of the triangle, not 7/8" (2.2 cm). The half-square triangles you cut with this ruler will have a blunt point for easy alignment and will require less trimming. A half-square or quarter-square triangle ruler (which works similarly but allows cutting with the bias in the correct position) can be used to cut the triangles in What Goes Around, the Knit This and Stitch That bags, the RELAX cushion set, Always, the Make banner and Windswept.

THREADS

Match the thread to the fabric when piecing. For example, when using cotton fabric, use cotton thread. Avoid using polyester thread for patchwork—over time, the threads will wear differently and the polyester thread will cut through the fibers of the cotton.

Always use a fine, good-quality thread for your sewing machine. Your machine will produce less fluff by sewing with good-quality material, and your seams will lie flatter and last longer. In most situations, cream, white, or grey threads are appropriate for piecing—there is no need to change colors to match the fabrics you are sewing, but do match the value. If you are using a multicolored fabric, use a neutral-colored thread, such as beige or grey, which will blend into the background.

For appliqué I use Aurifil 80 weight cotton thread, which is very fine and helps to hide your stitches.

For hand quilting, I use Aurifil 12 weight cotton rather than traditional quilting thread. I like my stitches to stand out and make a statement, and I love the decorative element that thicker thread adds to the quilt. A thicker thread is much easier for beginners to handle because you can take larger stitches—up to ¼" (6 mm) in length—and you use a longer, thicker needle than for traditional quilting.

TECHNIQUES

This section covers the principal techniques used in this book. Some are techniques you may never have tried before, while others are techniques that I might approach a little differently. I recommend reading this section carefully before starting any of the projects in this book.

HALF-SQUARE TRIANGLES

There are different ways to cut and piece half-square triangles. The projects in this book are written using the most common technique for half-square triangles, which is to cut a square, and then cut the square on one diagonal into two triangles. The triangles are then sewn into pairs along the diagonals using a ¼" seam. As a result, the cutting instructions include ⅞" for the seam allowances. For example, if 2⅞" squares are cut into half-square triangles and then joined in pairs, the size of the resulting unit will be 2½" square (2" finished). Because the diagonal edges are on the bias, they will be prone to stretching when stitching and pressing, so handle with care. If you use a different method, be sure to cut the pieces so they will finish at the correct size and adjust the cut quantities as needed to fit the technique.

CONSTRUCTING YOUR QUILT

If an assembly diagram is provided, be sure to refer to it as well as to the photograph. Many quilt designs, especially complex ones using more than one type of block, feature optical illusions caused by the way in which the various components are combined. Sometimes the logic of the quilt's construction will not become clear, until you look at an assembly diagram.

ADDING BORDERS OR LONG STRIPS

Borders may be added for decorative effect or to increase the quilt's size, or both. They may have squared-off or mitered corners. The quilt pattern will tell you what length to cut the borders, but you should always measure your quilt top before cutting the border fabric and then adjust the length of the border strips if necessary.

To get a true measurement, measure in both directions through the center of the quilt rather than along the edges. This is because the edges may have distorted a little during the making of the quilt, especially if any of the edge pieces are bias-cut.

Use these measurements to calculate the length of each border. When pinning them to the quilt top, be sure to pin for the full length of the borders, matching the centers and both ends first—this is important to keep the borders flat.

TYPES OF BATTING

Some types of batting need to be quilted closer together than others to prevent them from drifting around within the quilt or fragmenting when washed. Polyester batting requires less quilting than cotton or wool batting. However, some polyester battings have a tendency to fight the sewing machine. Wool battings provide more warmth and comfort than polyester battings. However, they require denser quilting, and those that are not needle-punched, tend to pill. Needle-punched wool blends are more stable and require less dense quilting.

Cotton battings require quilting as much as every ½"–3" (12mm–7.5 cm). Needle- punched cotton battings are more stable and can be quilted up to 10" (25 cm) apart. Ask your favorite quilt store for advice if you are unsure which batting to choose for your project.

MAKING THE BACKING

The batting and backing should be at least 4" (10 cm) larger all around than the quilt top. Allow more if using a longarm quilting machine. You may need to join multiple widths of fabric, or add a strip of scraps or leftover blocks, to obtain a large enough piece for the backing. Press any seams in the backing open to reduce bulk when quilting. If you need to join two pieces of batting, butt them up together without overlapping, and zigzag stitch by machine across the join.

ASSEMBLING THE LAYERS

Press the quilt top and backing fabric. Lay the backing fabric right side down on a large, flat, clean surface (preferably one that is not carpeted). Smooth it out carefully and then tape it to the surface using masking tape. Tape it at intervals along all sides, but do not tape the corners, as this will cause the bias to stretch out of shape. Place the batting on top of the backing fabric and smooth it out. Center the well-pressed quilt top, right side up, on top of the batting, ensuring that the top and backing are square to each other. Smooth out.

BASTING

Once you have assembled the three layers, you need to baste them together before quilting. Basting can be done with safety pins if machine quilting or with long hand stitches if hand quilting. If you are using safety pins, prior to machine-quilting, start from the center of the quilt and pin through all three layers at intervals of about 8" (20 cm). Make sure the pins are kept away from the lines to be quilted. Once the quilt is basted, it can be moved. Do not use safety pins if you are hand quilting as the pins prevent the hoop from sitting evenly.

To baste if you are using hand stitches, baste the whole quilt both horizontally and vertically, always working from the center out, using long hand stitches at intervals of about 6" (15 cm). Using a curved needle is a good idea, as this makes the task easier on the wrists. Do not use this basting method if you intend to quilt by machine, as the basting threads will get caught under the presser foot.

Some machine quilters offer a machine basting service. This can be a worthwhile investment and save you many hours of tedious preparation.

Remove the basting stitches or safety pins only when all the quilting has been completed.

QUILTING

Quilting can be fairly rudimentary, with its main purpose being to hold together the layers of the quilt, or it can be decorative and sometimes extremely elaborate. Machine quilting is quick, but nothing beats hand quilting for sheer heirloom beauty and a soft hand to the finished quilt.

Designs for hand quilting, or elaborate designs for machine quilting, are generally marked on the quilt top before the quilt's layers are sandwiched together. On pale fabric, the marking is done lightly with a regular or chalk pencil. On dark fabrics, a chalk pencil or a Hera marker should be used to create creases.

Pencil lines can be erased later. Be very light and cautious with your marking, because even the faintest lines can sometimes be difficult to remove. Free-flowing lines can be drawn on, but if you intend to quilt straight lines or a cross-hatched design, use masking tape to mark the lines on the quilt top. Such tape comes in various widths, from ¼" (6 mm) upward.

If you intend to outline-quilt by machine, you may be able to sew straight enough lines by eye. If not, you will need to mark the quilt top first, or use your machine foot as a guide.

HAND QUILTING

Quilting by hand produces a softer line than machine-quilting and will add to the lovingly handmade quality of a quilt. I prefer to quilt using Aurifil 12 weight cotton or Perle cotton, since these stand out vividly against the fabric's surface and create a wonderful texture. However, traditional waxed quilting thread can be used if you prefer.

To quilt by hand, the fabric needs to be held in a quilting hoop. Large freestanding frames are available, but hand-held ones are less expensive, more portable, and just as effective. One edge of a hand-held frame can be rested against a table or bench to free up both hands. The hoop should fit your arm from the crook of your elbow to the base of your fingers, NOT the size of your quilt top. Most people will use a 14" hoop.

Hand quilting, like machine quilting, should commence in the center of the quilt and proceed outward. Place the plain (inner) ring of the frame under the center of the quilt. Position the other ring, with the screw, over the top of the quilt to align with the inner ring. Tighten the screw so that the fabric in the frame becomes taut, but not drum-tight.

For traditional quilting, choose the smallest needle that you feel comfortable with. (These needles are known as "betweens.") For quilting with Perle cotton or 12 weight cotton which is what I prefer, use a good-quality crewel embroidery needle (my favorite is a no. 9).

with the middle or index finger of your dominant hand until you can feel the tip of the needle resting on your finger at the back (use a metal thimble to make this easier).

3 Without pushing the needle through, rock it back to the top of the quilt and use your underneath finger to push the tip up. Put your upper thumb down in front of the needle tip while pushing up from the back, as shown. This will make a small "hill" in the fabric.

4 Push the needle through the fabric. This makes one stitch. To make a row of several stitches, push the needle along to the required stitch length, then dip the tip into the fabric and repeat the above technique. Gently pull the stitches to indent each stitch line evenly. You should always quilt towards yourself, as this reduces hand and shoulder strain, so turn the quilt in the required direction.

TIP *You can protect your underneath finger using a stick-on plastic shield such as a Thimble-It.*

1 Thread the needle with about 18" (46 cm) of thread. Knot the end of the thread with a one-loop knot. Take the needle down through the quilt top into the batting, a short distance from where you want to start quilting. Tug the thread slightly so that the

knot pulls through the fabric into the batting, making the starting point invisible.

2 With your dominant hand above the quilt and the other beneath, insert the needle through all three layers at a time at a 90-degree angle,

NEEDLETURN APPLIQUÉ

There are various appliqué techniques, but I always use my needleturn method. If you wish to machine-appliqué your letters, you don't need to add the seam allowance and you can cut around each shape right along the traced silver gel line. I also recommend using a fusible to prevent fraying and puckering under your machine.

SILVER GEL PENS

These are reflective on any fabric and when you are stitching, it's easy to see whether you have turned your shape under neatly. If you can still see the silver color, you haven't got the shape quite right. Often the marking wears off as you stitch. Some brands of ink may not work out so be careful. The ink isn't guaranteed to wash out. Mine always have, but you never know. Be careful with that tracing! Be sure to buy a gel pen that is meant for scrapbooking. They will say 'acid free', or 'archival quality'.

1 Place the template on the right side of the fabric and trace around it with a silver gel pen. (Fig. 1)

Figure 1

2 Cut around the outside of the appliqué a scant ¼" (6 mm) from the gel line. Finger-press along the line all around the shape, including into any curves or points. The 'S' in the first row of the Windswept project is a fairly easy shape, but it is essential to finger press along the gel pen line all the way around the perimeter, even into the curves, before sewing.

TIP *Finger pressing is not pressing the seam under and making it stay—rather, it is just a firm pinch along the gel line to make a crease. This gives the fabric a memory. When you are sewing, the fabric already knows where you want it to go and it is easier to manipulate. Especially for the Back to Black Alphabet, finger pressing is ESSENTIAL to successful needleturn appliqué. Don't be tempted to use an iron instead. A finger-pressed line is easy to manipulate, whereas an ironed line is difficult to change if you iron a point into a crease or a line in the wrong spot (not to mention the fact that you'd be very likely to burn your fingers!). Finger-pressed creases act as the perfect guide to help you turn the fabric as you sew.*

3 Position the appliqué on the Background fabric, using the positioning tools provided in your pattern.

4 Instead of pins, I use liquid appliqué glue to fix the appliqué temporarily onto the Background fabric. If you glue all the appliqué shapes onto a quilt top, then you can carry it around with you, without worrying whether the pins have come out. You only need a few dots of glue on each shape to make them stick. Leave a few minutes for the glue to dry. Don't worry if the glue smudges, as it can be easily removed later or washed off. I don't use a glue stick for this—wiping the stick across the bias shapes for appliqué can distort the fabric very easily and make it difficult to stitch flat. (Fig. 2)

Figure 2

5 Use a milliners needle with coordinating thread which is knotted at the end. Always match the color of your appliqué thread to the color of the fabric that you are appliquéing, not to the background. I use very long, fine, milliners needles, also known as straw needles, for my appliqué. The finer the needle, the smaller you can make your stitches for invisible appliqué. (Fig. 3)

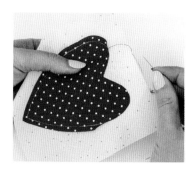

Figure 3

6 Begin stitching anywhere on the shape, but preferably not at an inside curve or a point. Come through from the wrong side of the background fabric with the needle, to the right side of the background fabric, catching the outermost finger-pressed edge of the appliqué shape.

7 Go down into the background fabric right next to where you came up. Run your needle along at your desired spacing on the wrong side of the background fabric, and come up once more, catching the edge of the appliqué shape.

> **TIP** *Don't try to turn the whole edge under before you sew it; just turn under the small section you are working on. This makes it easier to keep track of the gel-pen line and ensures accurate stitching around the shape.*

8 Sew all around the edge of the appliqué in this manner. The stitches should just catch the edge of the appliqué fabric and be small and fairly close together. This will both make the appliqué strong to prevent it being torn and keep the shape from looking puckered. Tie the thread off on the wrong side of the background fabric with a small knot.

9 To stitch a sharp point, sew all the way to the very tip of the gel pen line and give the thread a sharp tug. Sweep all the fabric at the point around in an arc underneath the tip of the shape, spreading it out underneath the appliqué. Tug the thread again to make the point sharp, and continue stitching. (Fig. 4)

Figure 4

10 To stitch an inside point or curve, clip the seam allowance all around the curve and back to the gel pen line, about ¼" (6mm), or just once on a 'V' point. Use the needle to sweep the fabric away from you to prevent fraying. On a 'V' point, place three small stitches right at the point, spread (like a birds foot), to hold the seam in place.

11 To prevent bulk, turn the Background fabric with the wrong side facing up and use a sharp pair of small-tipped scissors to make a small cut behind the appliqué, taking care not to cut it or the stitches. I do this only on shapes or areas that are larger than 1", so it is not needed on the thin parts of the letters. Cut away the background fabric underneath the appliqué leaving a ¼" seam allowance (6 mm) away from the sewn lines. Although this step is not strictly necessary, it makes the appliqué sit nicely and creates fewer layers to quilt through, especially where appliqué pieces overlap. Repeat this process for each shape.

TIP *If you are attaching multiple layers, remove the fabric from behind each piece before stitching the next appliqué shape.*

APPLIQUÉING BIAS CURVES

1 With a pencil, lightly mark the curve of the appliqué onto the background fabric.

2 At the ironing board, position one end of the bias strip on the beginning of the drawn line from Step 1. Position the tip of the iron onto the end of the bias strip. In a gradual smooth and gentle movement, pull the bias strip away from the iron aligning it as best you can on the center of the pencil line and following closely with the tip of the iron.

TIP *If you have a strip longer than the ironing board, iron as far as you can go along the curve and stop.*

3 Lift the bias strip up carefully and put dots of glue along the pencil line, then replace the strip and let it dry. Shift the background fabric along the ironing board and repeat until you have glued the bias strip to the background and come to the end of your drawn pencil line.

MAKING BIAS STRIPS

Bias strips are used in appliqué for making vines or stems for flowers, basket handles, and the like. Bias tape is used in the Rainbow cushion (page 102). You can buy it pre-made, but it's good to know how to make your own. The strips need to be cut on the bias (45-degree angle to the straight-of-grain) so that they can be easily ironed and glued into a curve without puckering. Fat quarters are useful for making bias strips, as they yield a good length for small projects and are a manageable size.

1 Trim a fat quarter to 18″ square. Using the 45-degree angle line on your patchwork ruler, make a diagonal cut. Maintaining the same angle on the ruler, cut parallel strips that are ½" (12mm) wider than you want the finished bias strip to be.

2 To join the cut strips, place them perpendicular to each other, right sides together, and sew on the angled short edge. Add strips until it is as long as you require. Trim the seam allowances to a scant ¼", and press the seams open to reduce the bulk when stitching.

3 Using a Hera marker, score a line ¼" (6mm) from the edge on both long sides of the strip all the way along the length.

4 At the score lines, fold over the length of the strip with the wrong sides together. Carefully press the edges of the strip along both lines.

ADDING A LABEL

Once you have finished your quilt, consider adding a label so that future generations will know who made it—especially if the quilt is a gift. Pre-printed fabric labels are available to buy, or you could simply write on a nice piece of coordinating fabric with a laundry marker and slipstitch it to the back of the quilt.

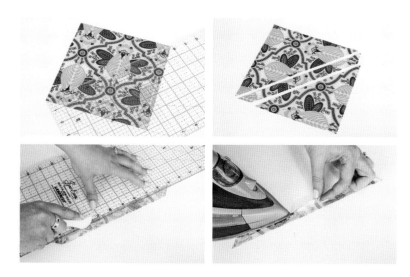

RESOURCES

I'm a big fan of shopping at my local quilt shop. Where possible, I would always encourage you to shop at your local patchwork shop rather than buy online. I'm aware that this isn't always feasible but a local quilt shop will help you select your fabric, give you recommendations and hints, and offer great classes to help you along the way. They can't survive to hold your classes unless you also shop with them, and so many are going out of business as a result of online shopping. I am often asked about my favorite Aussie quilt shops, so here they are. I have taught at them all, so if you stop in, be sure to say 'Hi' from me! Viva la Quilt Shop!

AUSSIE QUILT SHOPS
- Millrose Cottage in Ballan, VIC
- Steph's Patchwork in Moruya, NSW
- Precious Time in Toowoomba, QLD
- Amitié Textiles in Melbourne, VIC

FABRIC ONLINE
Listing a quilt shop close to everyone is not possible, so here are a few online shops I like (they ship worldwide).

Unusual print and text fabric online
- Polka Dot Tea
  www.etsy.com/au/shop/
  PolkaDotTeaFabrics
- Pink Castle Fabrics
  www.pinkcastlefabrics.com
- Fabricworm
  www.fabricworm.com
- Hawthorne Threads
  www.hawthornethreads.com
- Sunny Day Supply
  www.sunnydayfabric.com
- Miss Matatabi
  www.etsy.com/au/shop/
  MissMatatabi

Interesting solid fabrics online
- Oakshott
  www.oakshottfabrics.com
- Rowan Shot Cottons
  www.gloriouscolor.com

Liberty fabrics online
Liberty, is beautiful for patchwork and especially for appliqué. Many shops stock a good range these days—my favorite in Australia is The Strawberry Thief.
- www.thestrawberrythief.com.au

In North America, try Duck a Dilly.
- www.duckadilly.com

NOTIONS (HABERDASHERY)
I am often asked what brands I use. There are thousands of great products out there, but these are the brands I prefer at the moment.

For appliqué
- Tulip Milliners needles #11
- Aurifil 80 weight cotton
- Roxanne Glue-Baste-It appliqué glue

For quilting
- Tulip Crewel Embroidery needles #10
- Aurifil 12 weight cotton
- Clover open-sided thimble
- Opie quilting hoop
- Matilda's Own 100% cotton batting (wadding)

Acrylic/Perspex rulers and template sets

- Template sets are available for the WINDSWEPT quilt here and quilts in my previous books. In addition, I sell the tools mentioned for appliqué and quilting, including Australian-made quilting hoops, my fabric ranges for Lecien, Spotlight, and Windham Fabrics, my thread collections for Aurifil, scrap bags, and all my books.

- Everything I recommend is also available through my website www.sarahfielke.com — and yes, I ship worldwide!

FIND ME ONLINE

I love answering questions and hearing from those of you who have made my quilts or enjoyed my books. Come and say hi!

Website: www.sarahfielke.com
Blog: www.thelastpiece.net
Email: sarah@sarahfielke.com
Twitter: @sarahfielke
Facebook: /sarah.fielke
Pinterest: sarahfielke
Instagram: @sfielke

See my blog at www.thelastpiece.net for free video tutorials on Perfect Circle Appliqué, Making Bias Strips, and Hand Quilting. You can take an online class with me in appliqué and using specialty rulers at www.craftsy.com.

My Block of the Month (BOM) programs run every year. The programs include a full video tutorial for every step of the quilt. You can sign up for the current BOM or buy the pattern for a previous one at www.sarahfielkeblockofmonth.com

TEACHING

I teach regular classes in Sydney, and I often teach interstate and overseas. I teach online classes at blueprint.com.

You can find all the details of my latest classes at my blog or email me to ask for details if you would like me to visit your local shop or group.

ACKNOWLEDGMENTS

Thanks must go to:

Damo. Can't be done without him.

Sue Stubbs, photographer extraordinaire and sometime quilt wrangler, who understands me and my quilts so wonderfully well.

Kat Jones of Two Cats Quilts, for doing such a stunning job on the machine quilting and being so willing, available and open to ideas! You can find Kat and her beautiful work at www.twocatsquilt.com.au or on Instagram @twocatsquilts

Windham Fabrics for sending wonderful parcels of fabrics that have been worked into my designs. My mate T, and Free Spirit Fabrics for the Tula Pink All Stars.

Susanne, Rae Ann, Kari, Alison and Shea at Lucky Spool for their help, support, design, editing and all-around wonderfulness! I'm so excited to make this book with all of you.

Flo Tynan, maker of excellent cushions and drinker of my gin. Thanks Frenchie xx

Dave and Cath for the use of their beautiful home and their beautiful daughter!

Miss Jillie, Elyse, Brandon and Elle for their expert modeling skillz.

Charlie and Oscar, just for existing.

All of my beautiful quilty peeps far and near, my friends, my students, online, in my BOMs and those I've never met. Your enthusiasm for my designs and seeing you interpret them is what keeps me going.

TEMPLATES

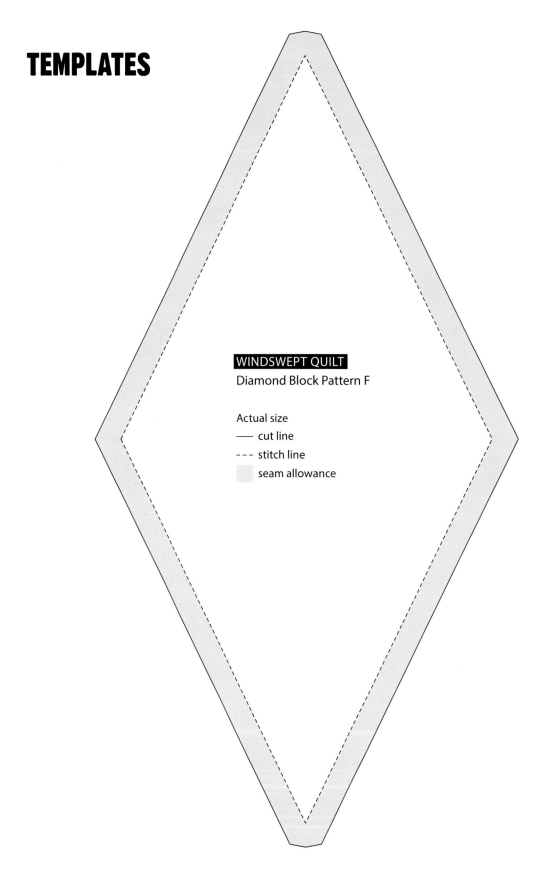

WINDSWEPT QUILT

Diamond Block Pattern F

Actual size

—— cut line

- - - stitch line

seam allowance

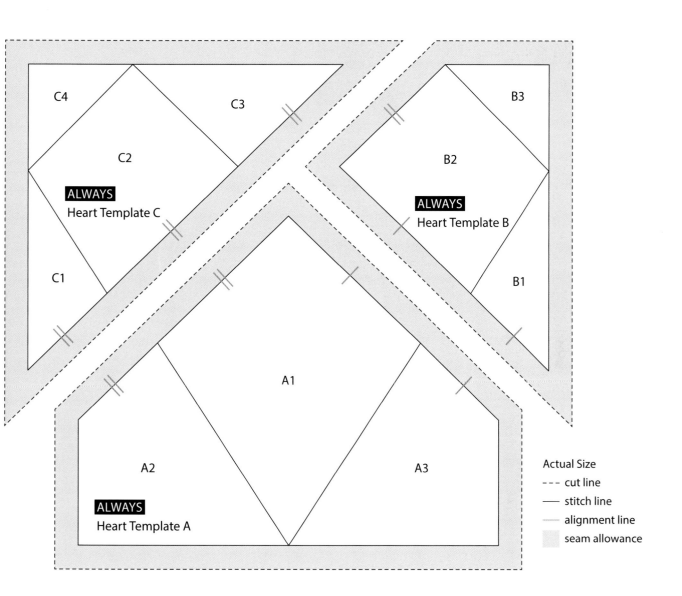

C4

C3

C2

B3

ALWAYS
Heart Template C

B2

ALWAYS
Heart Template B

C1

B1

A1

Actual Size
- - - cut line
—— stitch line
—— alignment line
▨ seam allowance

A2

A3

ALWAYS
Heart Template A

STITCH THAT BAG

Pattern B

Enlarge 130%

—— cut line

- - - stitch line

seam allowance

STITCH THAT BAG

Pattern C

Enlarge 130%

—— cut line

RAINBOW SCRIPT CUSHION
Dot Template A

Actual Size
—— cut line
--- stitch line
▨ seam allowance

RAINBOW SCRIPT CUSHION
"rainbow" pattern

Enlarge 200% and join at lines, aligning triangles

center crease

center crease

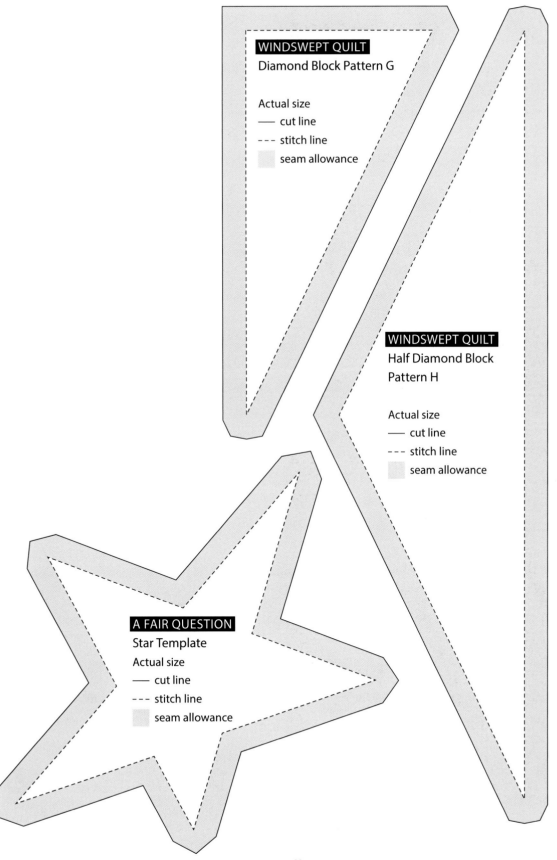

WINDSWEPT QUILT
Diamond Block Pattern G

Actual size
— cut line
- - - stitch line
■ seam allowance

WINDSWEPT QUILT
Half Diamond Block
Pattern H

Actual size
— cut line
- - - stitch line
■ seam allowance

A FAIR QUESTION
Star Template
Actual size
— cut line
- - - stitch line
■ seam allowance

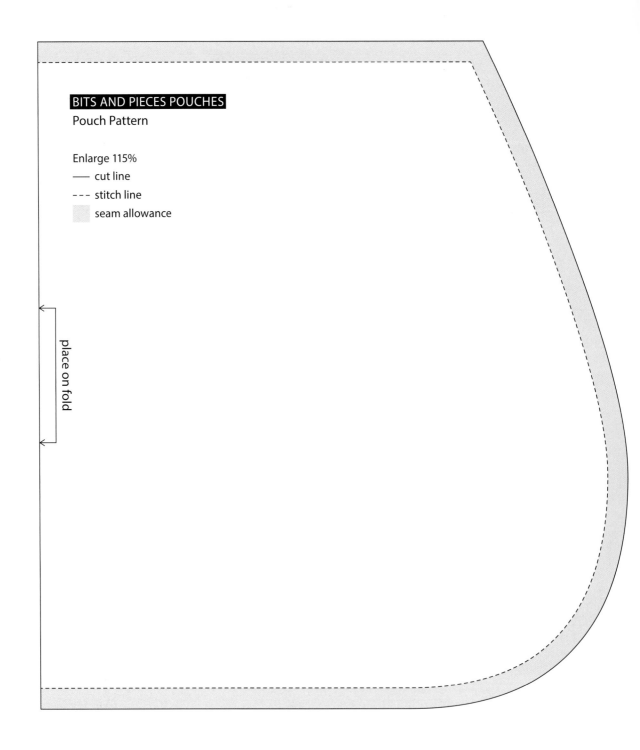

BITS AND PIECES POUCHES
Pouch Pattern

Enlarge 115%

—— cut line

--- stitch line

▢ seam allowance

place on fold

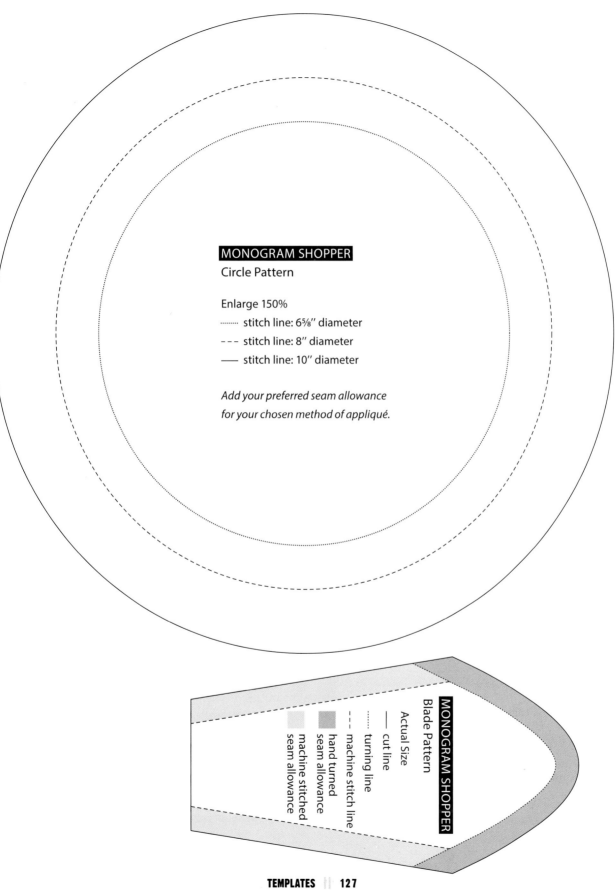

MONOGRAM SHOPPER
Circle Pattern

Enlarge 150%

·········· stitch line: 6⅝'' diameter

- - - stitch line: 8'' diameter

—— stitch line: 10'' diameter

Add your preferred seam allowance
for your chosen method of appliqué.

MONOGRAM SHOPPER
Blade Pattern

Actual Size

—— cut line

·········· turning line

- - - machine stitch line

machine stitched seam allowance

hand turned seam allowance

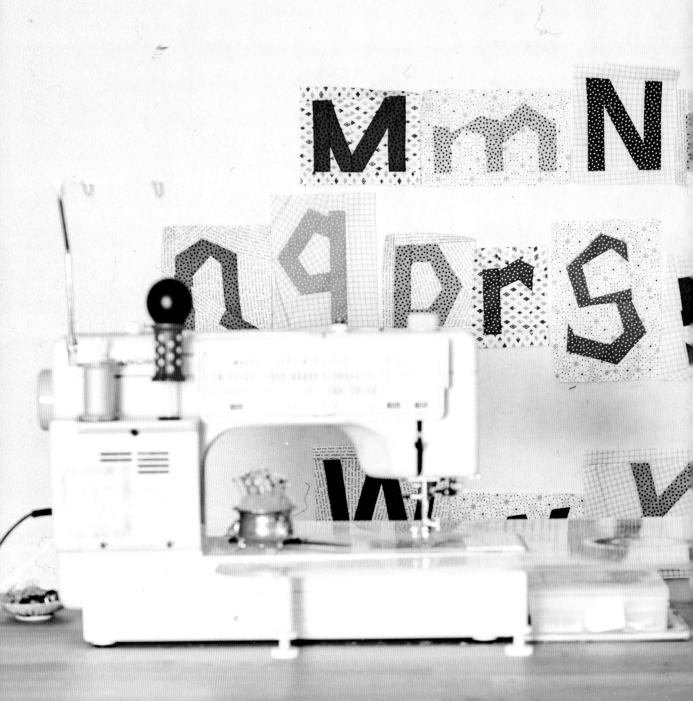